WORKING WITH FAMILIES

I0792814

Family Breakup and Survival

Workbook

Reproducible Activities to Address the Challenges Families Face Today

By Ester R. A. Leutenberg
& John J. Liptak, EdD

wholeperson
Health & Wellness Publishers
Duluth, Minnesota

wholeperson
Health & Wellness Publishers

101 West 2nd Street, Suite 203
Duluth, MN 55802

800-247-6789

books@WholePerson.com
WholePerson.com

Family Breakup and Survival Workbook
Facilitator Reproducible Activities for Groups and Individuals

Printed in the United States of America

10 9 8 7 6 5 4 3 2 1

Editorial Director: Carlene Sippola
Art Director: Mathew Pawlak

Library of Congress Control Number: 2015917443
ISBN: 978-157025-342-3

Family Breakup and Survival Workbook

In this workbook, the title **CARE-GIVER** and **ADULTS** will be used for family members or paid helpers who give direct CARE and are responsible in any way for one or more children and/or teens.

Throughout the workbook, the term **BREAKUP** will be used inclusively of any breakup, separation, annulment, and/or divorce.

What is a Care-Giver Breakup?

A care-giver breakup is one of the most stressful events that a family could encounter. Separation, and ultimately a breakup, can be very difficult on both care-givers, children, and other caring family members.

It is important to distinguish among the various types of circumstances that are included as breakups in this workbook. Here are a few:

- A couple dating.
- A legal separation, which often comes before a divorce.
- Annulment, when a marriage is declared null and void.
- Divorce, the dissolution of marriage and the changing of legal responsibilities.
- Separation in which a couple stops cohabitating.

Breaking up can mean many different things to different people. For the purposes of this workbook, we are using the term *breakup* to include people living in the above situations. Breakups are extremely complicated processes that usually involve phases of a breakup between the two people and their families, and then possible various stages of a grieving process, for all concerned.

Although some breakups end with a reconciliation, the stages of grief, the trauma, the issues of child-care, the communications, the visitations, the relationships, the feelings, and the changes still disrupt the family unit in a heart-breaking way. Things that are said, family members remember. Children suffer. How they react depends on their age, personality and the circumstances of the separation process. Families change. The contents of this workbook will help, whether there is a reconciliation or not.

The next two sections will provide information related to these two important aspects of any breakup.

The Phases of a Breakup

It is never easy to break up with someone, but the breakup of a relationship can thrust your world into chaos and trigger all types of painful and negative feelings. The process of a relationship breakup follows some fairly distinct and predictable phases.

This model is not meant to be a definitive way that people in a relationship progress toward a breakup. All breakups will be unique and specific to the people involved. Therefore, the model that follows is designed to provide you with a sense of the behaviors, thoughts, and feelings that accompany each of the phases of a breakup.

Phase 1

In this phase, the idea of a breakup often surfaces. The relationship experiences stress and it feels like it is in trouble by the initiator, or by both people. The notion of a breakup is often not directly verbalized, but may be verbalized also.

Phase 2

In this phase, ideas about a breakup are often verbalized. Typically, there is an initiator and a non-initiator. The initiator often has gone through a gamut of feelings and is now focusing on the cognitive aspects of telling the partner. The non-initiator usually feels rejected, anger, confusion, self-doubt and depression.

Phase 3

In this phase, the couple involved in the breakup usually begin to shut down and distance themselves physically from each other. They may stop talking to each other and doing things for each other. The couple involved at this point often look at what happened and who is at fault.

Phase 4

In this phase, the legal process often begins. This tends to be a more cognitive stage than the previous one, and most difficult when children are involved. The couple in the relationship feel the reality that is setting in and they begin to explore how their roles, and their families' lives will be different.

The phases of a breakup can be devastating to everyone involved in the relationship. It is important to remember how stressful each of these phases are for both the initiator and the non-initiator as they consider how it affects themselves, each other, children, and other family members.

Stages in Grieving a Breakup

Regardless of their makeup and family dynamics, all members of a family proceed through specific stages in the process of grieving a breakup.

Although the descriptors for these stages may differ from what others use, they are simply a guide for better understanding the general issues that family members may experience while going through a breakup. They are not absolute or chronological.

Stage 1 (Denial)

In this stage, family members pretend that the breakup is not a big deal and that they can easily move on with their lives. They often talk about their situation and their emotions until the initial shock wears off. Most people in this stage may feel numb about the situation and try to move past it quickly.

Stage 2 (Anger)

In this stage, after the initial pain begins to wear off, family members begin to become angry about their situation or others involved in the breakup. They get angry and see themselves as victims of an injustice. In this stage, the anger can range from mild feelings of aggravation to feelings of rage. In this stage family members may often search for ways to vent their anger.

Stage 3 (Bargaining)

In this stage, family members try different tactics to get back what they had. They begin to believe that a reconciliation, no matter how bad the situation was, is better than living the way they did in the past, or living the way they are currently. They often seek a "quick fix" for the situation so that they can get back to the way life was before, even if it was not ideal. In this stage, many members of the family may feel guilty about what happened.

Stage 4 (Sadness)

In this stage, family members begin to experience signs of sadness, possibly leading to depression. They may have difficulty sleeping, lose interest in eating, feel exhausted, and are often irritated. In this stage, family members feel pensive and wish the relationship had turned out differently.

Stage 5 (Moving On)

In this stage, family members begin to accept the fact that a breakup might be the best for all people in the relationship, and they are ready to move on. They are interested in releasing the past, living in the moment, and making strides toward a fulfilling future. They realize that it is time to move on and focus on the positivity in their lives.

Stage 6 (Release & Establishment)

In this stage, family members are ready to release any bitterness and even accept the reality of the situation. They are ready to begin establishing new relationships that will be part of a positive future.

Stress & Fear Related to a Breakup

Stress will accompany any breakup of two caregivers. This stress is often experienced as fear, and fear is often masked as anger, jealousy, frustration and many other emotions. However, stress and fear can cause overwhelming, debilitating emotions that people involved in a breakup experience. Fear and stress often come to care-givers in a breakup in the form of worry and anxiety about the unknown future. Following are some of the possible triggers of fear and stress:

- How can I take care of the children myself?
- What if I am unable to see my children anymore?
- How will I earn enough money to support myself and/or my children?
- How will I pay the bills? Will I need to go back to work and/or get a second job?
- Who will care for the children or drive them where they need to go when I am working?
- How will I manage by myself?
- What if my children are taken from me?
- Who will want to be in a relationship with me? Will I meet someone else?
- When will I have time to date?
- What if the children don't like who I am dating?

Although this is a short list of concerns, it demonstrates the types of thoughts that might be triggering stress and fear in the care-givers who have had a breakup, or are about to break up. It is important that care-givers take steps to face their fears about breaking up and learn how to manage the stress associated with a breakup. Care-givers must find ways to cope with the fear and stress related to a breakup. **Coping is a process by which people manage their lives and heal after a breakup.** Coping means actively managing stress that could grow significantly more extreme over time. When care-givers begin to experience stress that can potentially become a crisis, they must rely on a variety of coping resources and mechanisms:

- **Cognitive Strategies** present ways that individual family members can alter their perceptions of stressful events. Strategies include reframing the problem, thinking positively, and recognizing the need to change their negative and irrational thinking.
- **Self-Care** allows one to take care of self in the midst of change. Some strategies include:
  - o Take time each day to nurture yourself: *(example: massage, book, walk in the park, yoga class.)*
  - o Develop a new routine to deal with the uncertainty and chaos that surrounds life after a breakup.
  - o Don't make any major decisions for a while after the breakup. *(Example: moving or quitting a job.)*
  - o *Develop new interests. (Example: new activities that you did not do in the past.)*
- **Emotion Expression and Management** suggests that it's okay to experience the wide variety of emotions that accompany any breakup. Care-givers need to have, express, and manage these emotions.
- **Management of Your Life** teaches that even though you have experienced a breakup, you still have a bright future. Some strategies include:
  - o Maintain effective family communication.
  - o Avoid overanalyzing the past or getting stuck in negative feelings of the past.
  - o Develop new dreams based on your new situation.
  - o Get out and meet new people and cultivate new friendships.
  - o Spend time with people who support and value you as a person.
- **Get support** by sharing your feelings with other family members and friends. You should not have to go through this alone. *(Example: support group that includes others in similar situations. If none, start one!)*
- **Grieving**, in and of itself, is a healing process that can help care-givers to let go of their old relationship and move on.

In order to maintain an effective and useful family unit, family members must develop skills for managing change, coping with stress, and building resiliency from external and internal stressors.

Family Breakup & Survival Workbook Contents

This workbook contains the materials facilitators need to work with changes that occur in the family structure due to a breakup.

Each chapter contains six primary elements:

1) A set of skills to be gained from completion of the assessments and activities by all family members.
2) A set of assessments to help children/teens gather information about themselves in a focused situation.
3) A set of assessments to help children/teens gather their perceived information about how the other family members feel in a shared and focused situation.
4) A set of assessments to help care-givers or other adults gather information about themselves in a focused situation.
5) A set of assessments to help care-givers or other adults gather their perceived information about how the other family members feel in a shared and focused situation.
6) A set of guided self-exploration activities to help all of the participants to process information and learn ways to build a stronger family unit.

Assessments are valuable tools for facilitators to help with building a healthy family unit:

- Understand and predict future behavior.
- Identify the nature of problems and explore possible solutions.
- Explore the family as a system, rather than focusing on individual behaviors.
- Identify the family constructs, patterns, structure, and level of functioning.
- Develop hypotheses (with the help of the facilitator) about the issues most often interfering with positive family dynamics.
- Explore family members' perceptions of the various issues affecting their family.
- Identify their areas of strength as a family.

Through the assessment process, facilitators will be better able to join with the family members, provide support, offer feedback, validate issues and concerns, understand and appreciate each other's perceptions and feelings, enhance family strengths, and generate hope for the future.

Assessments in Each Chapter

Family members often need to work together on issues they are experiencing in their household. However, before effective, therapeutic discussions can take place, family members need vehicles with which they can explore and categorize their thinking about their current family life. Assessments are a valuable method for collecting important information about members of a family and can provide a vehicle with which family members can tell their narratives safely. Assessments also provide family members and the facilitator with different perspectives held by various family members. Therefore, assessments are included for facilitators to use in examining family relationships, functions, constructs and dynamics.

Each chapter of this workbook begins with four different reproducible assessments, scoring instructions, and interpretation guides that can be easily used with all members of the family with whom you are working. As the facilitator, you may choose to use any combination of assessments that represent the family dynamics of your current clients. You may choose to use one assessment, two, three, or all four, depending on the make-up of the family and the number of people in the family with whom you are working.

Photocopy as many pages of each as you need for each participant.

(Continued on the next page)

Family Breakup & Survival Workbook Contents *(Continued)*

The assessments related to the topics covered in each chapter will include the following:

Assessment #1: One assessment for each child to identity personal feelings about the stressful changes occurring in the family.

Assessment #2: One assessment for each child to identify perceptions of one or more of the children's/teens' caregivers: (parent, grandparent, relative, group-home parent, etc.) about the stressful changes in the family. Each member's perceptions of the others' feelings are vitally important for them to understand and empathize with them.

Assessment #3: One assessment for each adult (children's/teens' caregivers: parent, grandparent, relative, group-home parent, etc.) to identify their own feelings about the stressful changes in the family.

Assessment #4: One assessment for each adult (children's/teens' caregivers: parent, grandparent, relative, group-home parent, etc.) to identify perceptions of each child about the stressful changes in the family. Each member's perceptions of the others' feelings are vitally important for them to understand and empathize with them.

Assessments are critical in working with families experiencing change, stress, and maybe even crisis. The assessments contained in this workbook provide family members with valuable information about themselves and their perceptions of each other. Assessments in this workbook are different from traditional assessments because they are designed for all members of the family, not just the care-givers or just the children or teens.

Qualitative vs. Quantitative Assessments

This workbook contains *self-assessments* and *not tests.* Assessments derive specialized, focused information about family members and family dynamics.

1) These assessments help identify patterns of behavior and attitudes which are productive and unproductive in a family setting. The purpose of these assessments is not to find fault with any family members; the assessments are designed to guide self-discovery and inform family members.
2) Some assessments measure knowledge or right or wrong responses. These assessments are designed to help family members explore their current family dynamics, not yield right or wrong answers. These assessments ask only for opinions or attitudes about topics related to their family life.
3) Some assessments often have formal ways for family members to compare their scores with others who have taken the same assessments. These assessments are based on self-reported data. In other words, the accuracy and usefulness of the information is dependent on the information that participants honestly provide about themselves. All scores will simply be compared with the scores of other members of the family.
4) Some assessments are designed to be administered by a facilitator. The assessments in this workbook are designed to be administered, scored, and interpreted by the participants with the help of the facilitator as a starting point to begin to learn more about themselves and their behavior within the family structure. Remind participants that the assessments are exploratory exercises and not final measurements of functioning.

When family members are completing, scoring and interpreting the assessments contained in this workbook, please be aware that the assessments are not a substitute for professional assistance. If you feel any of the members of the family with which you are working need more assistance than you can provide, please refer them to an appropriate professional.

(Continued on the next page)

Family Breakup & Survival Workbook Contents *(Continued)*

Guided Self-Exploration Activities

Guided self-exploration activities assist all family members in self-reflection to identify effective family behaviors as well as ineffective family behaviors. Guided self-exploration is designed to help family members make a series of discoveries about themselves and other members of the family. These insights will help family members realize that a family is much more than the sum of its individual parts.

These brief, easy-to-use self-reflection tools are designed to promote insight and self-growth. The activities in this workbook are also related to the assessments so that you can identify and select activities quickly and easily. Many different types of guided self-exploration activities are provided for you to pick and choose the activities most needed by your family members and that will be most appealing to them.

The GUIDED-SELF-EXPLORATION ACTIVITIES can take TWO DISTINCT FORMS:

1. Writing, list-making and journaling activities for **care-givers, older children and teens.** These types of activities encourage older family members to be introspective and write about their experiences.
2. Any of the handouts can be adapted by the facilitator for use with **children or teens (depending on their age and/or maturity level)** by asking them to draw, doodle, or respond about the situation represented on the handout. This will provide an opportunity for them to express themselves in ways they are able.

The unique features of self-guided exploration activities make them usable and appropriate for a variety of individual sessions and family sessions.

Features of Guided Self-Exploration Activities

- **Quick, easy and rewarding to use** – These guided self-exploration activities are designed to be an efficient, appealing method for motivating family members to explore information about themselves - including their thoughts, feelings, actions and relationships - in a relatively short period of time.
- **Reproducible** – Because the guided self-exploration activities can be reproduced by the facilitator, no more than one book needs to be purchased. You may photocopy as many items as you wish for your participants. If you want to add or delete words on a page, make one photocopy, white out and/or write your own words, and then make photocopies from your personalized master.
- **Participative** – These guided self-exploration activities help family members to quickly focus their attention, aid them in the self-reflection process, and guide them to learn new and more effective ways of interacting with each other.
- **Motivating** – Because they can be completed by all members of the family, these guided self-exploration activities are designed to help all family members feel empowered to face the issues confronting the family and to learn ways for the family to be a more cohesive unit.
- **User-friendly** – The guided self-exploration activities are user-friendly, and family members will feel motivated and self-empowered after completing these activities.
- **Adaptable to a variety of family situations and dynamics** – The guided self-exploration activities can be used with a variety of today's families and can be tailored to meet the needs of the families with whom you work.
- **Focused** – Each guided self-exploration activity is designed to focus on a single set of coping issues that families typically face.
- **Flexible** – The guided self-exploration activities are flexible and can be used independently or to supplement other types of interventions.

The Working with Family Series

As the structure of families has changed, so has the need for new tools, techniques and resources with which facilitators can assist family members.

The purpose of this series of workbooks is to provide a tool for practitioners who work with families in need of help and/or intervention, and to identify family members' issues through qualitative assessments as well as activities designed to overcome these problems.

This workbook series is unique in that all of the assessments and activities are designed for all members of the family, not exclusively for children, for teens or for care-givers.

The assessments and activities in this workbook and others in this series will allow family members to accomplish the following:

- Know, understand and empathize with each other better, and accept and celebrate differences in family members. This will provide family members the tools they need to work together to blend more effectively.
- Develop a greater feeling of bonding and interacting in positive ways, with the common goal that family members genuinely care for one another in nurturing ways.
- Accept each individual family member as a unique and valued person.
- Provide support and comfort to each other to enhance a sense of trust, loyalty and respect for each other.
- Communicate honestly with each other, resolve conflicts, and compromise and negotiate for their desires and needs.

~~~~~~

The next page is for your participants!

As they are ready to begin the assessments in this workbook, it is necessary to convey to the participants the instructions on the page, *For the Participants* (page xi).

- **You may photocopy one for each participant.**
- **You may read it to the participants.**
- **They can read it to themselves.**
- **Different volunteers can read each bullet point aloud.**

~~~~~~

For the Participants

**You are about to start a new adventure,
to learn more about yourself, your family and your home life.
You will use assessments and self-exploration activities.**

- Because there is no time limit for completing the assessments, you can work at your own pace. Allow yourself time to reflect on your results, how they compare to what you already know about yourself, and what other family members have said about you.
- Other members of your family may be taking the same or similar assessments. Some assessments are designed to help you explore your feelings about your family life, and some will ask for your perceptions of other family members. *Your responses will show how you are aware of, understand, or interpret the thoughts, feelings, and actions of these family members.*
- Do not answer the assessments as you think other family members would like you to answer them. These assessments are for your personal reflections on your family life and to help you to explore some issues that may be keeping your family from being as close, comfortable and content as possible.
- Assessments are powerful tools, but only if you are honest with yourself. Take your time and be truthful in your responses so that your results are an honest reflection of *you.* Your level of commitment in completing the assessment honestly will determine how much you learn about yourself and your home environment.
- If you are going to complete two assessments, be sure to read the instructions. The assessments have similar formats, but they have different scales, responses, scoring instructions, and methods for interpretation.
- Remember that learning about yourself in your home and family life, as well as in relation to other members of your family, is designed to promote your growth as well as the growth of everyone in your family unit.

**Enjoy taking the assessments and discovering your results.
Respond in an honest and open way.**

It may sometimes be difficult to admit the truth, or to hear the truth from someone else, but an open forum for communication is part of the process to learn as much about yourself and your home/family environment as you can.

In this workbook, the title CARE-GIVER or ADULTS will be used for family members or paid helpers who give direct care and are responsible in any way for a child or teen.

Throughout the workbook, the term BREAKUP will be used inclusively for any breakup, separation, annulment, and/or divorce.

Chapter Topics

The *Family Breakup & Survival Workbook* is designed to be used either independently or as part of an integrated curriculum. You may administer any of the assessments and the guided self-exploration activities to an individual or multiple family members with whom you are working, or you may administer any of the activities over multiple sessions. Feel free to pick and choose those assessments and activities that best lead to the outcomes you desire. The assessments and activities are divided into four chapters to help you identify and select assessments easily and quickly.

Chapter I: Communication
This chapter helps family members explore the way information about the breakup was conveyed to them.

Chapter II: Visitation and Relationships
This chapter helps family members explore how visitation is being handled by both parents and how relationships with the family care-givers are progressing.

Chapter III: Feelings
This chapter helps family members explore how well they are managing their current family stress and explore ways to cope more effectively with change and stress.

Chapter IV: Changes
This chapter helps family members explore the various changes that have resulted because of the breakup, and how family members are dealing with those changes.

Thanks to these professionals who make us look good!

Editorial Director – Carlene Sippola
Cover Design & Art Director – Mathew Pawlak

Editor and Lifelong Teacher – Eileen Regen, M Ed, CJE
Reviewer and Proofreader – Jay Leutenberg, CASA
Reviewer and Behavioral Skills Expert – Carol Butler, MS Ed, RN, C
Reviewer and Educator – Niki Tilicki, MAED
Teen Counselor – Eileen Jonaitis, MAED

Table of Contents – **Introduction**

Chapter I – **Communication**

Chapter II – Visitation and Relationships

Chapter III – **Feelings**

Chapter IV – **Changes**

CHAPTER 1

Communication

For the Facilitator

Explanation of the Four Scales in this Chapter

As the facilitator, you may choose any combination of assessments that will work for each of the particular families with whom you are working.

You may choose to use one scale or all of them, depending on the make-up of the family and the number of people in the family.

Photocopy as many of each as needed.

1. **One for each child/teen** to identify personal feelings
2. **One for each child/teen** to identify perceptions of care-giver's feelings
3. **One for each adult** to identify personal feelings
4. **One for each adult** to identify perceptions of children's or teens' feelings

You will need to photocopy the corresponding Introduction and Directions for each scale you administer.

Chapter I – *Communication* Skills

These skills are behavioral objectives which family members will meet as they engage in the assessments and guided self-exploration activities.

Children/Teens

Self-assess, score, and interpret personal communication, and perception of care-givers' communication about the breakup on three scales: explanation, message, and availability.

Detail the day one found out about the breakup including the location, level of surprise, people present and absent, feelings, and reactions.

Identify information received and withheld about the breakup's cause, who is/is not at fault, what will stay the same, what will change, living arrangements, financial and other considerations. Note different messages from different people and with whom to talk about inconsistencies.

Share concerns about visitation, continued love by both care-givers, irrational self-blame, and other related issues, by identifying how one is affected and with whom to process feelings.

Care-Givers

Self-assess, score, and interpret personal communication, and perception of children/teens' communication about the breakup on three scales: explanation, message, and availability.

Describe what was told to three people about the breakup's cause, who is/is not at fault, what will stay the same, and what will change. Explain inconsistencies and with whom to speak about them.

Name family members who need reassurance, describe misunderstandings to address, and document a date to discuss the issues.

Share concerns about assuring the children they are loved, involvement in their activities, and related issues, by identifying the effects on self, family members, the family unit, and with whom to process feelings.

All Family Members

Compare individual results with other family members, and the family's total scores on three scales: explanation, message, and availability, related to communication about the breakup.

Depict and/or describe self before and after the breakup.

Identify positive and negative aspects of life before and after the breakup.

Create an "I want …" list upon acknowledgment that the breakup is definite.

List the advantages and disadvantages of the breakup.

Depict and/or describe the family's breakup, including ongoing changes and/or stress.

Personalize words of wisdom by sharing ways to heal, get back on track, and take small steps to break free and move forward.

Communication Scale

Introduction & Directions

Communicating the fact that your family will change due to a breakup can be difficult. Not knowing how each member of the family will react to this fact can be a challenge for everyone. Ongoing conversations may continue to be difficult. It is important for family members to have open communications.

This scale can help you explore how you and family members have communicated, or are presently communicating, about the breakup. This scale contains 18 statements. Read each of the statements and decide how descriptive each statement is of you or your family member. In each of the choices listed, circle the number of your response on the line to the right of each statement.

The responses may be different for each care-giver and child/teen.

Complete an assessment for each one.

In the following examples, the circled number 1 under "FALSE" indicates the statement is not true of the person completing the scale.

Scale # 1 (Responses)

	TRUE	FALSE
When communicating with this care-giver about the breakup ...		
I talk with loving words	2	(1)

Scale # 2 (Perceptions)

	TRUE	FALSE
When communicating with this care-giver about the breakup ...		
This care-giver talks with loving words	2	(1)

Scale # 3 (Responses)

	TRUE	FALSE
When communicating with this child or teen about the breakup ...		
I talk with loving words	2	(1)

Scale # 4 (Perceptions)

	TRUE	FALSE
When communicating with this child or teen about the breakup ...		
This child or teen talks with loving words	2	(1)

This is not a test and there are no right or wrong answers. Do not spend too much time thinking about your answers. Your initial response will be the most true for you. Be sure to respond to every statement.

(Turn to the next page and begin.)

SCALE #1

Child's/Teen's *Communication*

Child's/Teen's Name ______________________________ Date ____________

Care-Giver's Name ____

When communicating with this care-giver about the breakup ...	TRUE	FALSE
I talk with loving words	2	1
I am honest	2	1
I say how I feel in a loving way	2	1
I understand the situation	2	1
I listen without interrupting	2	1
I ask questions to better understand	2	1

E TOTAL = ________

When communicating with this care-giver about the breakup ...	TRUE	FALSE
I am able to express my feelings	2	1
I am able to understand others' feelings	2	1
I am open to further discussion	2	1
I am not defensive or argumentative	2	1
I express my thoughts with sensitivity	2	1
I am satisfied with how I was told	2	1

M TOTAL = ________

When communicating with this care-giver about the breakup ...	TRUE	FALSE
I am willing to discuss it with other family members	2	1
I appreciate how the situation was explained to me	2	1
I am okay with the situation	2	1
I am "there" for this care-giver	2	1
I am honest about my concerns of the changes to come	2	1
I show that I still love this care-giver	2	1

A TOTAL = ________

SCALE #1
Child's/Teen's *Communication* Scoring Directions

Child's/Teen's Name ________________________ Date ____________

Care-Giver's Name ________________________

This scale is designed to measure your communications with your care-giver. For the sections you just completed, add the numbers that you circled. You will get a total in the range from 6 to 12 for each one. Transfer these totals to the spaces below. Then add your three scores to get your Grand Total.

E **Explanation** Total = ________

M **Message** Total = ________

A **Availability** Total = ________

GRAND TOTAL = ________

Profile Interpretation

Scale Score	Grand Total	Result	Indications
6 to 7	18 to 23	Low	Low Scores indicate that you do not have an effective way of communicating about the breakup with the above stated care-giver.
8 to 10	24 to 30	Moderate	Moderate Scores indicate that you have a fairly effective way of communicating about the breakup with the above stated care-giver.
11 to 12	31 to 36	High	High Scores indicate that that you have an effective way of communicating about the breakup with the above stated care-giver.

Scale Descriptions

Explanation – The child or teen scoring High on this scale communicates about the breakup in an open way, responds with loving honesty, is available, asks appropriate questions, and is open, direct and honest.

Message – The child or teen scoring High on this scale communicates about the breakup, is kind, not defensive, listens attentively, and expresses the pain being experienced.

Availability – The child or teen scoring High on this scale communicates about the breakup, reacts in a positive and loving way, understands others' feelings, honestly expresses concerns about changes expected in the future.

GRAND TOTAL – The child or teen scoring High on these scales seems to be able to communicate at ease with the above stated care-giver.

SCALE #2

Child's/Teen's Perception of a Care-Giver's *Communication*

Child's/Teen's Name ________________________________ Date ______________

Care-Giver's Name ____

When communicating with this care-giver about the breakup …	TRUE	FALSE
This care-giver explains with loving words	2	1
This care-giver is honest	2	1
This care-giver expresses feelings in a loving way	2	1
This care-giver understands the situation	2	1
This care-giver listens without interrupting	2	1
This care-giver asks questions to better understand	2	1

E TOTAL = ________

When communicating with this care-giver about the breakup …		
This care-giver is able to express feelings	2	1
This care-giver is able to understand others' feelings	2	1
This care-giver is open to further discussion	2	1
This care-giver is not defensive or argumentative	2	1
This care-giver expresses thoughts with sensitivity	2	1
This care-giver told about the breakup in a kind way	2	1

M TOTAL = ________

When communicating with this care-giver about the breakup …		
This care-giver is willing to discuss it with all family members	2	1
This care-giver appreciates how the situation was explained to me	2	1
This care-giver is okay with the situation	2	1
This care-giver is "there" for me	2	1
This care-giver is honest about my concerns of the changes to come	2	1
This care-giver shows me that I am still loved	2	1

A TOTAL = ________

SCALE #2
Child's/Teen's Perception of a Care-Giver's *Communication* Scoring Directions

Child's/Teen's Name ________________________ Date ____________

Care-Giver's Name ________________________

This scale is designed to measure your perception of your care-giver's communications with you. For the sections you just completed, add the numbers that you circled. You will get a total in the range from 6 to 12 for each one. Transfer these totals to the spaces below. Then add your three scores to get your Grand Total.

E Explanation **Total =** ________

M Message **Total =** ________

A Availability **Total =** ________

GRAND TOTAL = ________

Profile Interpretation

Scale Score	Grand Total	Result	Indications
6 to 7	18 to 23	Low	Low Scores indicate that this child or teen does not believe that the above stated care-giver has an effective way of communicating about the issues of the breakup.
8 to 10	24 to 30	Moderate	Moderate Scores indicate that this child or teen believes that the above stated care-giver has a fairly effective way of communicating about the issues of the breakup.
11 to 12	31 to 36	High	High Scores indicate that this child or teen believes that the above stated care-giver has a very effective way of communicating about the issues of the breakup.

Scale Descriptions

Explanation – The child or teen scoring High on this scale believes that this care-giver communicates information about the breakup in an open way, responds with loving honesty, is available, asks appropriate questions, and is open, direct and honest.

Message – The child or teen scoring High on this scale tends to believe that when this care-giver communicates information about the breakup, it is with kindness and empathy, not defensive, listens attentively, and expresses and understands the pain being experienced.

Availability – The child or teen scoring High on this scale tends to believe that when this care-giver communicates about the breakup, the person reacts in a positive and loving way, understands the feelings and honestly expresses concerns about the changes expected in the future.

GRAND TOTAL – The child or teen scoring High on these scales seems to be receiving excellent support from this care-giver.

SCALE #3

Care-Giver's *Communication*

Care-Giver's Name ______________________________ Date ______________

Child's/Teen's Name ______________________________

When communicating with this child or teen about the breakup ...	TRUE	FALSE
I talk with loving words	2	1
I am honest	2	1
I say how I feel in a loving way	2	1
I understand the situation	2	1
I listen without interrupting	2	1
I ask questions to better understand	2	1

E TOTAL = ________

When communicating with this child or teen about the breakup ...	TRUE	FALSE
I am able to express my feelings	2	1
I am able to understand others' feelings	2	1
I am open to further discussion	2	1
I am not defensive or argumentative	2	1
I express my thoughts with sensitivity	2	1
I am satisfied with how I was told	2	1

M TOTAL = ________

When communicating with this child or teen about the breakup ...	TRUE	FALSE
I am willing to discuss it with other family members	2	1
I feel good about the way I explain the situation	2	1
I am okay with the situation	2	1
I am "there" for this child or teen	2	1
I am carefully honest about my concerns of the changes to come	2	1
I demonstrate that I still loved this child or teen	2	1

A TOTAL = ________

SCALE #3
Care-Giver's *Communication*
Scoring Directions

Care-Giver's Name ____ Date ______________

Child's/Teen's Name ____

This scale is designed to measure your communications with your child or teen. For the sections you just completed, add the numbers that you circled. You will get a total in the range from 6 to 12 for each one. Transfer these totals to the spaces below. Then add your three scores to get your Grand Total.

E Explanation **Total** = ___________

M Message **Total** = ___________

A Availability **Total** = ___________

GRAND TOTAL = ___________

Profile Interpretation

Scale Score	Grand Total	Result	Indications
6 to 7	18 to 23	Low	Low Scores indicate that you do not have an effective way of communicating about the breakup with the above stated child or teen.
8 to 10	24 to 30	Moderate	Moderate Scores indicate that you have a fairly effective way of communicating with your child or teen about the breakup.
11 to 12	31 to 36	High	High Scores indicate that that you have an effective way of communicating with your child or teen about the breakup.

Scale Descriptions

Explanation – The care-giver scoring High on this scale communicates about the breakup with the above stated child or teen in an open way, responds with loving honesty, is available, asks appropriate questions, and is open, direct and honest.

Message – The care-giver scoring High on this scale communicates about the breakup with the above stated child or teen in a kind, not defensive way, listens attentively, and expresses the pain being experienced

Availability – The care-giver scoring High on this scale communicates about the breakup with the above stated child or teen in a positive and loving way, understands feelings, and honestly expresses concerns about the changes expected in the future.

GRAND TOTAL – The care-giver scoring High on this scale seems to be able to communicate at ease with the above stated child or teen.

SCALE #4

Care-Giver's Perception of a Child's/Teen's *Communication*

Care-Giver's Name ______________________________ Date ______________

Child's/Teen's Name ____

When communicating with this child or teen about the breakup ...	TRUE	FALSE
This child or teen talks with loving words	2	1
This child or teen is honest	2	1
This child or teen expresses feelings in a loving way	2	1
This child or teen understands the situation	2	1
This child or teen listens without interrupting	2	1
This child or teen asks questions to better understand	2	1

E TOTAL = ________

When communicating with this child or teen about the breakup ...	TRUE	FALSE
This child or teen is able to express feelings	2	1
This child or teen is able to understand others' feelings	2	1
This child or teen is open to further discussion	2	1
This child or teen is not defensive or argumentative	2	1
This child or teen expresses thoughts with sensitivity	2	1
This child or teen was told about the breakup in a kind way	2	1

M TOTAL = ________

When communicating with this child or teen about the breakup ...	TRUE	FALSE
This child or teen is willing to discuss it with all family members	2	1
This child or teen appreciates how the situation was explained	2	1
This child or teen is okay with the situation	2	1
This child or teen is "there" for me	2	1
This child or teen is honest about concerns of the changes to come	2	1
This child or teen demonstrates that I am still loved	2	1

A TOTAL = ________

SCALE #4
Care-Giver's Perception of a Child's/Teen's *Communication*
Scoring Directions

Care-Giver's Name ____________________ Date __________

Child's/Teen's Name ____________________

This scale is designed to measure your perception of your child or teen's communications with you. For the sections you just completed, add the numbers that you circled. You will get a total in the range from 6 to 12 for each one. Transfer these totals to the spaces below. Then add your three scores to get your Grand Total.

E Explanation Total = __________

M Message Total = __________

A Availability Total = __________

GRAND TOTAL = __________

Profile Interpretation

Scale Score	Grand Total	Result	Indications
6 to 7	18 to 23	Low	Low Scores indicate that this care-giver does not believe that the above stated child or teen has an effective way of communicating about the issues of the breakup.
8 to 10	24 to 30	Moderate	Moderate Scores indicate that this care-giver believes that the above stated child or teen has a fairly effective way of communicating about the issues of the breakup.
11 to 12	31 to 36	High	High Scores indicate that this care-giver believes that the above stated child or teen has a very effective way of communicating about the issues of the breakup.

Scale Descriptions

Explanation – The care-giver scoring High on this scale believe that this child or teen communicates information about the breakup in an open way, responds with loving honesty, is available, asks appropriate questions, and is open, direct and honest.

Message – The care-giver scoring High on this scale tends to believe that when this child or teen communicates information about the breakup, it is with kindness and empathy, not defensive, listens attentively, and expresses and understands the pain being experienced

Availability – The care-giver scoring High on this scale tends to believe that when this child or teen communicates about the breakup, the person reacts in a positive and loving way, understands the feelings and honestly expresses concerns about the changes expected in the future.

GRAND TOTAL – The care-giver scoring High on these scales seems to be receiving excellent support from this child or teen.

Communication Scale
Family Score Totals

For each of the items on the scales, insert the person's name completing the scale, and transfer each person's scale on one line below. This form can be helpful in allowing family members to compare their own results.

Scale 1 Name (Child's/Teen's Scale)	Score Explanation	Score Message	Score Availability	TOTAL SCORE
Example: *John*	*8*	*11*	*9*	*28*

Scale 2 Name (Child's/Teen's Perception of Care-giver Scale)	Score Explanation	Score Message	Score Availability	TOTAL SCORE

Scale 3 Name (Care-giver's Scale)	Score Explanation	Score Message	Score Availability	TOTAL SCORE

Scale 4 Name (Care-giver's Perception of Child's/Teen's Scale)	Score Explanation	Score Message	Score Availability	TOTAL SCORE

The Day You Found Out about the Breakup

(Child or Teen)

Think back to the event, and how and when you found out.

Where were you at the time?

Who was present?

Who was not present?

How did you find out?

Were you surprised? Why or why not?

How did you feel?

How did you react?

What Was Told to Other People about the Breakup

(Care-Giver)

Often different things are told to different people.
Journal three different conversations.

Person ______________________ **Relationship** ______________________

What I said about breaking up. ______________________

What I said was the cause of the breakup. ______________________

____

What I said about who is or is not at fault. ______________________

____

What will stay the same. ______________________

What will change. ______________________

Person ______________________ **Relationship** ______________________

What I said about breaking up. ______________________

What I said was the cause of the breakup. ______________________

____

What I said about who is or is not at fault. ______________________

____

What will stay the same. ______________________

What will change. ______________________

Person ______________________ **Relationship** ______________________

What I said about breaking up. ______________________

What I said was the cause of the breakup. ______________________

____

What I said about who is or is not at fault. ______________________

____

What will stay the same. ______________________

What will change. ______________________

If you were you consistent in what you said, why? ______________________

____

If you were inconsistent in what you said, why? ______________________

____

I Was, or Was Not, Told

(Child or Teen)

At times, children or teens are not told everything they want to know. Care-Givers usually have a good reason for this, however, it can bring up confused feelings. Put a √ below in the Told column if you were told, and an X if you were not.

About ...	Told (√)	What I was Told	Wasn't Told (X)	How I Found Out
Breaking-up				
The cause of the breakup				
Who is or is not at fault				
What will stay the same				
Where people will live and with whom				
What other changes will occur				
Finances				
Other				

What was told to you by one person that differed from what you were told by another person?

___

___

Who can you talk to about that?___

___

Reassurance

(Care-Giver)

For all involved, a breakup can feel like a loss of a life that was. It is important to reassure all family members that everything will be okay, straighten out any misunderstandings, and show unconditional love. In the spaces that follow, identify the family member, the misunderstandings and when you will do it.

Family Member	Misunderstanding I Need to Address	When?

My Worries

(Child or Teen)

During any breakup, family members usually experience a wide variety of worries. Complete the table below. Then make a promise to yourself to talk with the people you identify in the third column. They can be different people for different issues.

My Worry	How it Affects Me	Who Can I Talk to About This?
Whom will I live with? Will we be separated?		
Where will I live? Will I have to move?		
Which care-giver will I live with? Will I be able to see the other one?		
What's going to happen with my care-givers		
Do they both still love me?		
Did I do something wrong?		
Will we have enough money?		
How can I be sure that the breakup was not my fault?		
Other		
Other		
Other		

My Worries

(Care-Giver)

During any breakup, family members experience a wide variety of worries. These worries will disrupt a family unit. What are your worries about the breakup your family is experiencing? In the spaces below, identify your worries and how they affect you, and how your worries affect members of your family

My Worry	How it Affects Me	How My Worry Affects Our Family as a Whole or Individually
What's going to happen to the children?		
When will I see the children?		
Where will I live?		
How can I assure the children that I love them and will always love them?		
How do I stay involved with all of their activities.		
What is going to happen financially?		
How can I assure the children that the breakup was not their fault?		
Other		

With whom can you talk about your worries?

____

____

ME - Before the Breakup

The way you think about yourself often changes as a result of stressful times. In the box, write about, list words, phrases, and/or pictures that describe the way you were before the breakup.

What were the positive aspects of your life before the breakup?

____

____

What were the negative aspects of your life before the breakup?

____

____

ME - After the Breakup

The way you think about yourself often changes as a result of stressful times. In the box, write about, list words, phrases, and/or pictures that describe the way you were after the breakup.

What were the positive aspects of your life after the breakup?

___

___

What were the negative aspects of your life after the breakup?

___

___

What I Want

List what you want, now that the breakup has been decided on or has happened. Examples might include: from a child or teen, "I want you both involved in my life …" or from a care-giver, "I want to continue being a part of your lives…"

I want …

Advantages and Disadvantages

What do you see as the advantages of the breakup?

1.____
2.____
3.____
4.____
5.____
6.____
7.____
8.____
9.____
10.____

What do you see as the disadvantages of the breakup?

1.____
2.____
3.____
4.____
5.____
6.____
7.____
8.____
9.____
10.____

Reflecting Back

Telling the story of the process your family has gone through during a breakup can be helpful! Often family members want to deny or minimize the aspects of the breakup. A great way to tell your story safely is by writing it out or drawing pictures of it. In the space that follows, write or draw in as much detail as possible about the changes and stressors that are occurring in your family. Use the back of this page if you need additional space.

When We Suffer a Loss ...

When we suffer a loss, a break up, a painful change in our lives, we need to remember to take all the time we need to heal emotionally. Moving forward and getting back on track with our lives doesn't take a day. It takes a lot of small steps to allow us to break free from our broken self and move on.

~ Unknown Source

What small steps do you need to take to get back on track?

CHAPTER II

Visitation and Relationships

For the Facilitator

Explanation of the Four Scales in this Chapter

As the facilitator, you may choose any combination of assessments that will work for each of the particular families with whom you are working.

You may choose to use one scale or all of them, depending on the make-up of the family and the number of people in the family.

Photocopy as many of each as needed.

1. **One for each child/teen** to identify personal feelings
2. **One for each child/teen** to identify perceptions of care-giver's feelings
3. **One for each adult** to identify personal feelings
4. **One for each adult** to identify perceptions of children's or teens' feelings

You will need to photocopy the corresponding Introduction and Directions for each scale you administer.

Chapter II – *Visitation and Relationships* Skills

These skills are behavioral objectives which family members will meet as they engage in the assessments and guided self-exploration activities.

Children/Teens

Self-assess, score, and interpret personal feelings and behavior, and perception of care-givers' feelings and behavior on two scales: visitation and relationships.

Describe ways to make visitations meaningful, and note the benefits of each.

Draw activities one wants to do with specific family members, and note who can expedite them.

Identify ways and reasons one wants or does not want specific care-givers involved in one's life.

Care-Givers

Self-assess, score, and interpret personal feelings and behavior, and perception of children/teens' feelings and behavior on two scales: visitation and relationships.

Create a visitation schedule that defines living arrangements and ways to split or share time.

Identify who will make decisions about discipline, education, dating, activities, medical care, etc.

Document a parenting plan that designates responsibilities and potential problems regarding school, recreation, vacations, appointments, transportation, finances, etc.

Respond to a list of communication strategies to use in the presence of children. Note the other care-giver's reaction when one does or does not use active listening, assertiveness, negotiation, etc.

All Family Members

Compare individual results with other family members, and the family's total scores on two scales: visitation and relationships.

Write what one wants to say, explain why words are unspoken, and note with whom to process whether, and how, to express the thoughts and feelings.

Identify likes and dislikes about visitations with specific family members.

Describe thoughts, feelings, and actions related to visitations.

Visitation and Relationships Scale
Introduction & Directions

In a breakup, a parenting plan and visitation schedule must be developed for how the children will be cared for and where they will live. This plan is critical in providing children with information about how their time will be spent with each parent.

This scale explores how you and your family are coping with your crises. Read each of the statements and decide whether or not the statement describes you. This assessment contains 20 statements. Read each of the statements and decide how descriptive each statement is of you. In each of the choices listed, circle the number of your response on the line to the right of each statement.

Examples

Scale # 1 and # 3 (Individual's responses)

In the following example, the circled number 2 under "YES" indicates the statement is descriptive of the person completing the scale.

Regarding visitations with my care-giver ...	**YES**	**NO**
I like to get home on time	(2)	1

Regarding my relationship with this care-giver	**YES**	**NO**
I tell my care-giver what I need and want.	(2)	1

Scale # 2 and # 4: (Individual's perceptions)

In the following example, the circled number 1 under "NO" indicates the person who is completing the scale believes that this statement is not descriptive of the other family member.

Regarding visitations, I believe this care-giver knows that ...	**YES**	**NO**
I like to get home on time	2	(1)

Regarding our relationship, this care-giver ...	**YES**	**NO**
I tell this care-giver what I need and want.	2	(1)

This is not a test and there are no right or wrong answers. Do not spend too much time thinking about your answers. Your initial response will be the most true for you. Be sure to respond to every statement.

(Turn to the next page and begin.)

SCALE #1

Child's/Teen's *Visitation and Relationships*

Child's/Teen's Name ______________________________ Date ______________

Care-Giver's Name ____

Regarding visitations with my care-giver ...	**YES**	**NO**
I like to get home on time	2	1
I like to know exactly where I am going.	2	1
I like to be included in planning the visits	2	1
I do everything I can to make sure that we enjoy our visits	2	1
I don't like to miss visits.	2	1
I don't need to be entertained every minute.	2	1
I don't like to be late for visitations	2	1
I don't like when visitation times are rescheduled	2	1
I do everything I can to make sure I am on time	2	1
I try not to let my care-giver's "stuff" get in my way	2	1

V TOTAL = ________

Regarding my relationship with this care-giver ...	**YES**	**NO**
I tell this care-giver what I need and want.	2	1
I don't complain about the other care-giver or siblings	2	1
I don't encourage this care-giver to talk about each other	2	1
I respect the way this care-giver treats me	2	1
I don't deliver messages to this care-giver	2	1
I am understanding with this care-giver.	2	1
I will not spy on this care-giver for the other one	2	1
I resolve my issues of this care-giver, with this care-giver	2	1
I will not let myself be put in the middle of both care-givers	2	1
I want to remain in touch with this care-giver's family members	2	1

R TOTAL = ________

SCALE #1
Child's/Teen's *Visitation and Relationships* Scoring Directions

Child's/Teen's Name ______________________________ Date ____________

Care-Giver's Name ____

The scale you just completed is designed to measure how time is being spent during visitations and how well you and your care-giver are getting along. For the items on the previous page, count the scores you circled. Put that total on the line marked TOTAL at the end of both the scales. Then, transfer your total on the spaces below.

V Visitation Total = __________

R Relationships Total = __________

Profile Interpretation - Visitation

Scale Score	Result	Indications
10 to 13	Low	Low scores indicate that you don't feel good, have not created boundaries, and do not look forward, to visitations with your care-giver.
14 to 16	Moderate	Moderate scores indicate that you seem to feel okay, have some boundaries, and don't mind your visitations with your care-giver.
17 to 20	High	High scores indicate that you feel good, have created your own boundaries, and look forward to visitations with your care-giver.

Profile Interpretation - Relationships

Scale Score	Result	Indications
10 to 13	Low	Low scores indicate that you do not have an effective relationship with the stated care-giver.
14 to 16	Moderate	Moderate scores indicate that you have a fair relationship with the above stated care-giver.
17 to 20	High	High scores indicate that you have a very good relationship with the above stated care-giver.

Scale Descriptions

Visitation – The child or teen scoring high on this scale has definite opinions and ways of ensuring that visitations run smoothly, are on time, and are not rescheduled. He or she allows boundaries and expectations to be known.

Relationships – The child or teen scoring high on this scale believes he/she is doing a great job of maintaining a good relationship with the above stated care-giver, stating needs and wants, and placing appropriate limits on conversations about the other care-giver.

SCALE #2

Child's/Teen's Perception of a Care-Giver's *Visitation and Relationships*

Child's/Teen's Name ______________________________ Date ______________

Care-Giver's Name ____

Regarding visitations, I believe this care-giver knows that ...	**YES**	**NO**
I like to get home on time	2	1
I like to know exactly where I am going.	2	1
I like to be included in planning the visits	2	1
I do everything I can to make sure that we enjoy our visits	2	1
I don't like to miss visits.	2	1
I don't need to be entertained every minute.	2	1
I don't like to be late for visitations	2	1
I don't like when visitation times are rescheduled	2	1
I do everything I can to make sure I am on time	2	1
I try not to let my care-giver's "stuff" get in my way	2	1

V TOTAL = ________

Regarding our relationship, I believe this caregiver ...	**YES**	**NO**
Tells me what he/she needs or wants	2	1
Doesn't complain about the other care-giver or kids	2	1
Doesn't encourage me to talk about my other care-giver	2	1
Treats me with respect.	2	1
Doesn't ask me to deliver messages to my other care-giver	2	1
Is understanding	2	1
Doesn't ask me to spy on my other care-giver.	2	1
Resolves any issues he/she has about me, with me	2	1
Doesn't put me in the middle of both care-givers	2	1
Wants me to remain in touch with all family members	2	1

R TOTAL = ________

SCALE #2

Child's/Teen's Perception of a Care-Giver's *Visitation and Relationships*

Scoring Directions

Child's/Teen's Name ______________________________ Date ______________

Care-Giver's Name ____

The scale you just completed is designed to measure how time is being spent during visitations and how well you and your care-giver are getting along. For the items on the previous page, count the scores you circled. Put that total on the line marked TOTAL at the end of both the scales. Then, transfer your total on the spaces below.

V Visitation **Total = ___________**

R Relationships **Total = ___________**

Profile Interpretation - Visitation

Scale Score	Result	Indications
10 to 13	Low	Low scores indicate that the child or teen believes the above-stated care-giver doesn't respect the way he or she would like the visitations to take place.
14 to 16	Moderate	Moderate scores indicate that the child or teen believes the above-stated care-giver only respects some of the ways he or she would like the visitations to take place.
17 to 20	High	High scores indicate that the child or teen believes the above-stated care-giver respects most or all of the ways he or she would like the visitations to take place.

Profile Interpretation - Relationships

Scale Score	Result	Indications
10 to 13	Low	Low scores indicate that the child or teen believes that the above stated care-giver doesn't respect his or her wants and needs concerning visitations.
14 to 16	Moderate	Moderate scores indicate that the child or teen believes that the above stated care-giver hardly respects his or her wants and needs concerning visitations.
17 to 20	High	High scores indicate that the child or teen believes that the above stated care-giver respects all or most of his or her wants and needs concerning visitations.

Scale Descriptions

Visitation – The child or teen scoring high on this scale has definite opinions and ways of ensuring that visitations run smoothly, are on time, and are not rescheduled. They allow their boundaries and expectations to be known.

Relationships – The child or teen scoring high on this scale believes that they are doing a great job of maintaining a good relationship with their stated care-giver, stating their needs and wants, and placing appropriate limits on conversations about the other care-giver.

SCALE #3

Care-Giver's *Visitation and Relationships*

Care-Giver's Name ______________________________ Date ______________

Child's/Teen's Name ______________________________

Regarding visitations with this child or teen ...	**YES**	**NO**
I like to get home on time	2	1
I like to know exactly where I am going.	2	1
I like to be included in planning the visits	2	1
I do everything I can to make sure that we enjoy our visits	2	1
I don't like to miss visits.	2	1
I don't need to be entertained every minute.	2	1
I don't like to be late for visitations	2	1
I don't like when visitation times are rescheduled	2	1
I do everything I can to make sure I am on time	2	1
I try not to let my "stuff" affect my child or teen	2	1

V TOTAL = ________

Regarding my relationship with this child or teen	**YES**	**NO**
I tell this child or teen what I need and want	2	1
I don't complain about the other care-giver or children	2	1
I don't encourage this child or teen to talk about the other care-giver.	2	1
I respect the way this child or teen treats me	2	1
I don't deliver messages to this child or teen	2	1
I am understanding with this child or teen	2	1
I do not ask this child or teen to spy on the other care-giver	2	1
I resolve my own issues of this child or teen, with this child or teen	2	1
I will not let my child ot teen be put in the middle of both care-givers	2	1
I want to remain in touch with this child or teen's family members.	2	1

R TOTAL = ________

SCALE #3
Care-Giver's *Visitation and Relationships* Scoring Directions

Care-Giver's Name ______________________________ Date ____________

Child's/Teen's Name ______________________________

The scale you just completed is designed to measure how well time is being spent during visitations and how well you and your child or teen are getting along. For the items on the previous page, count the scores you circled. Put that total on the line marked TOTAL at the end of both the scales. Then, transfer your total on the spaces below.

V Visitation **Total = ________**

R Relationships **Total = ________**

Profile Interpretation - Visitation

Scale Score	Result	Indications
10 to 13	Low	Low scores indicate that you don't feel good, have not created boundaries, and do not look forward, to visitations with your child or teen.
14 to 16	Moderate	Moderate scores indicate that you seem to feel okay, have some boundaries, and don't mind your visitations with your child or teen.
17 to 20	High	High scores indicate that you are feel good, have created your own boundaries, and look forward to visitations with your child or teen.

Profile Interpretation - Relationships

Scale Score	Result	Indications
10 to 13	Low	Low scores indicate that you do not have an effective relationship with the stated child or teen.
14 to 16	Moderate	Moderate scores indicate that you have a fair relationship with the stated child or teen.
17 to 20	High	High scores indicate that you have a very good relationship with the stated child or teen.

Scale Descriptions

Visitation – The care-giver scoring high on this scale has definite opinions and ways of ensuring that visitations run smoothly, are on time, and are not rescheduled. He or she allow boundaries and expectations to be known.

Relationships – The care-giver scoring high on this scale is doing a great job of maintaining a good relationship with the child or teen, stating needs and wants, and placing appropriate limits on conversations about the other care-giver.

SCALE #4

Care-Giver's Perception of a Child's/Teen's *Visitation and Relationships*

Care-Giver's Name ______________________________ Date ____________

Child's/Teen's Name ______________________________

Regarding visitations, I believe this child or teen knows that ...	**YES**	**NO**
I like to get home on time	2	1
I like to know exactly where I am going.	2	1
I like to be included in planning the visits	2	1
I do everything I can to make sure that we enjoy our visits	2	1
I don't like to miss visits.	2	1
I don't need to be entertained every minute.	2	1
I don't like to be late for visitations	2	1
I don't like when visitation times are rescheduled	2	1
I do everything I can to make sure I am on time	2	1
I try not to let my "stuff" affect my child or teen	2	1

V TOTAL = ________

Regarding our relationship, I believe this child or teen ...	**YES**	**NO**
Tells me what he/she needs or wants	2	1
Doesn't complain about the other care-giver or kids	2	1
Doesn't encourage me to talk about the other care-giver	2	1
Treats me with respect.	2	1
Doesn't ask me to deliver messages to the other care-giver	2	1
Is understanding	2	1
Knows he or she is not expected to spy on the other care-giver	2	1
Resolves any issues he/she has about me, with me	2	1
Doesn't put his or herself in the middle of both care-givers	2	1
Wants me to remain in touch with all family members	2	1

R TOTAL = ________

SCALE #4

Care-Giver's Perception of a Child's/Teen's *Visitation and Relationships*

Scoring Directions

Care-Giver's Name _______________________________ Date ____________

Child's/Teen's Name ____

The scale you just completed is designed to measure how well time is being spent during visitations and how well you and your child or teen are getting along. For the items on the previous page, count the scores you circled. Put that total on the line marked TOTAL at the end of both the scales. Then, transfer your total on the spaces below.

V Visitation **Total =** __________

R Relationships **Total =** __________

Profile Interpretation - Visitation

Scale Score	Result	Indications
10 to 13	Low	Low scores indicate that the care-giver believes the above-stated child or teen doesn't respect the way he or she would like the visitations to take place.
14 to 16	Moderate	Moderate scores indicate that the care-giver believes the above-stated child or teen only respects some of the ways he or she would like the visitations to take place.
17 to 20	High	High scores indicate that the care-giver believes the above-stated child or teen respects most or all of the ways he or she would like the visitations to take place.

Profile Interpretation - Relationships

Scale Score	Result	Indications
10 to 13	Low	Low scores indicate that the care-giver believes that the above stated child or teen doesn't respect his or her wants and needs concerning visitations.
14 to 16	Moderate	Moderate scores indicate that the care-giver believes that the above stated child or teen somewhat respects his or her wants and needs concerning visitations.
17 to 20	High	High scores indicate that the care-giver believes that the above stated child or teen respects all or most of his or her wants and needs concerning visitations.

Scale Descriptions

Visitation – The care-giver scoring high on this scale has definite opinions and ways of ensuring that visitations run smoothly, are on time, and are not rescheduled. He or she allows boundaries and expectations to be known.

Relationships – The care-giver scoring high on this scale believes that he or she is doing a great job of maintaining a good relationship with the above stated child or teen, stating their needs and wants, placing appropriate limits on conversations about the other care-giver.

Visitation & Relationships Scale
Family Score Totals

For each of the items on the scales, insert the person's name completing the scale, and transfer each person's scale on one line below. This form can be helpful in allowing family members to compare their own results.

Scale 1 Name (Child's/Teen's Scale)	Score Visitation	Score Relationships	TOTAL SCORE
Example: *John*	*12*	*15*	*27*

Scale 2 Name (Child's/Teen's Perception of Care-giver Scale)	Score Visitation	Score Relationships	TOTAL SCORE

Scale 3 Name (Care-giver's Scale)	Score Visitation	Score Relationships	TOTAL SCORE

Scale 4 Name (Care-giver's Perception of Child's/Teen's Scale)	Score Visitation	Score Relationships	TOTAL SCORE

Our Visitation Schedule

(Care-Giver)

Within any breakup, creating a visitation schedule can greatly enhance the stability experienced by both care-givers and children. There needs to be some agreement on where and when they will reside, and how their time will be split and shared.

Child's/Teen's Name	With Whom Will This Child or Teen Reside the Majority of the Time	How Time Will Be Split or Shared

Who and how will these decisions be made?

Decisions	Who Makes These Decisions and How Will they be Made
Dating	
Discipline	
Attendance and/or participation in games, concerts, etc.	
Vacation, Holidays, school trips, etc.	
Medical Care, Braces, Tattoos, etc.	
Other	
Other	

Care-Giver Plan

(Care-Giver)

Care-giver plans are designed to spell out the expectations for each of the care-givers in a breakup. All care-giving plans will be different, but the purpose of this activity is to help care-givers create a stable environment and develop a routine for their children, without it becoming an issue each time. It is important for care-givers to do this activity together.

Care-Giver Responsibilities	How We Can Handle This	Problems We Might Encounter
School homework/obligations		
School and extracurricular activities		
Recreational activities, sports, lessons, etc.		
Holidays, school vacations, family vacations, etc.		
Birthdays		
Finances on "extras"		
School and college costs		
Medical/Dental appointments		
Driving or lending the car to go to various places. Driving younger siblings.		
Clothing, Music, Trend choices		
Other		
Other		

Making Visitation Meaningful!

(Child or Teen)

It is important to make your visitations meaningful. To do so, there must be enough time for a quality visit, and a plan for how you will use your time visiting. In the spaces that follow, identify some ways that your visitations can be meaningful.

Ways My Visitations Could Be More Meaningful	What We Could Do…	How This Would Be Good for Me
Example: *I would like to spend time alone with dad without my brother.*	*Ride bicycles.*	*We could share personal thoughts.*
1.		
2.		
3.		
4.		
5.		
6.		

My Ideal Visit

(Child or Teen)

Children and teens often fantasize about what they believe would be the ideal visit with a care-giver or other family member on either side of the family. Draw some things you would like to do.

Family member's name ____________________	Family member's name ____________________
Family member's name ____________________	Family member's name ____________________

To whom can you talk to so these things can happen?

____

____

Things I Don't Say

In a breakup situation, you may have many things you want to say, but don't feel comfortable saying. Identify some of the things you want to say to a care-giver, sibling, child/teen, or any family member.

A

B

C

D

Which letter was the hardest to write about and why?______________________________

____

____

Why don't you say these things? ____

____

____

Who can help you to figure out whether to say them or not, and/or learn how you can say them without hurting anyone's feelings? ____

____

____

Ways I Want My Care-Givers Involved

(Child or Teen)

In the spaces that follow, identify the ways you do want (top half), and do not want (bottom half), each of your care-givers involved in your life. Photocopy a page for each care-giver. If other care-givers are involved in your life (siblings, grandparents, aunts, uncles, group home leaders, etc.) make a copy for them.

Care-giver's Name ______________________________

WAYS I WANT this care-giver involved in my life	WHY I WANT this care-giver involved in my life
______________________	______________________
______________________	______________________
______________________	______________________
______________________	______________________
______________________	______________________
______________________	______________________
______________________	______________________
______________________	______________________

WAYS I DO NOT WANT this care-giver involved in my life	WHY I DO NOT WANT this care-giver involved in my life
______________________	______________________
______________________	______________________
______________________	______________________
______________________	______________________
______________________	______________________
______________________	______________________
______________________	______________________
______________________	______________________

Care-Giver Communication Visitation Strategies

(Care-Giver)

Peaceful and strategic communication during visitations is critical in making children and teens feel that the visitation experience is meaningful. Following are some of the critical communication strategies that are important. Explore how well you are accomplishing them.

Care-givers Communication Strategies with Their Children/Teens Present	Do I Do This, or Not? Describe.	How My Ex Usually Reacts When I Do This.	How My Ex Usually Reacts When I DON'T Do This.
Ask for opinions.			
Be friendly, but assertive, if needed.			
Compromise if possible.			
Display positivity.			
Do not over-react.			
Exercise patience.			
Keep conversations focused on the children.			
Listen actively.			
Make requests, not demands.			
Negotiate if necessary.			
Smile. (You can do it!)			
Use good body language.			
Other			

Which are the hardest to do? Why? ____________________

____

Visitation Likes and Dislikes

(Child or Teen)

When it comes to visitations, you will probably like some things and dislike some things. Identify some of your likes and dislikes about your visitations with any of the members of your family.

Things I like when I visit with ______________________________

____

Things I like when I visit with ______________________________

____

Things I like when I visit with ______________________________

____

Things I like when I visit with ______________________________

____

Things I like when I visit with ______________________________

____

Things I do NOT like when I visit with ______________________________

____

Things I do NOT like when I visit with ______________________________

____

Things I do NOT like when I visit with ______________________________

____

Things I do NOT like when I visit with ______________________________

____

Things I do NOT like when I visit with ______________________________

____

Visitation Likes and Dislikes

(Care-Giver)

When it comes to visitations, you will probably like some things and dislike some things that the children, teens, or the other care-giver says or does. Identify some of your likes and dislikes about visitations.

Things I Like ...

Things I Dislike ...

Dear Journal

People going through a breakup need to allow themselves to experience what they are feeling by expressing it through writing or drawing. In the space below, journal or draw your feelings, thoughts, and/or actions about visitations.

CHAPTER III

Feelings

For the Facilitator

Explanation of the Four Scales in this Chapter

As the facilitator, you may choose any combination of assessments that will work for each of the particular families with whom you are working.

You may choose to use one scale or all of them, depending on the make-up of the family and the number of people in the family.

Photocopy as many of each as needed.

1. **One for each child/teen** to identify personal feelings
2. **One for each child/teen** to identify perceptions of care-giver's feelings
3. **One for each adult** to identify personal feelings
4. **One for each adult** to identify perceptions of children's or teens' feelings

You will need to photocopy the corresponding Introduction and Directions for each scale you administer.

Chapter III – *Feelings* Skills

These skills are behavioral objectives which family members will meet as they engage in the assessments and guided self-exploration activities.

Children/Teens

Self-assess, score, and interpret personal feelings, and perception of care-givers' feelings on four scales: depression, anger, fear, and guilt.

Care-Givers

Self-assess, score, and interpret personal feelings, and perception of children/teens' feelings on four scales: depression, anger, fear, and guilt.

All Family Members

Compare individual results with other family members, and the family's total scores on four scales: depression, anger, fear, and guilt.

Identify new opportunities related to family changes, and ways they will work out well. Point out the most significant opportunity and give reasons.

Describe feelings about the breakup and note that it is acceptable to have feelings.

Respond to descriptions of the stages of grief by noting which have been or are being personally experienced. State perceptions of the stages other family members are going through.

Respond to a list of emotions, by noting early warning signs and ways to reduce the feelings.

Own and name emotions by drawing the faces of feelings experienced most often or intensely. Identify with whom to share the feelings.

Describe situations in which negative emotions are experienced, and healthy ways to express the feelings.

Compare positive and negative thoughts about the breakup, the accompanying feelings, and ways in which life will be different.

Identify persons with whom to share feelings, ways to approach them, and ways they can help.

Complete sentence starters to describe feelings, circumstances, what one wants to do, what one would rather do, and other reactions to the breakup.

Identify warning signs of more serious emotional problems by sharing personal experiences related to a "red flag" list, and noting with whom to talk.

Describe honest feelings toward specific family members, reasons, ways to the express feelings, and requests to make of each family member. Discuss the difficulties of being honest.

Complete sentence starters to clarify guilt-related wishes, feelings, and regrets.

Identify illogical and negative thoughts, along with the accompanying feelings and actions. Point out trends, and document steps to reduce or change the thoughts that lead to negative emotions.

Feelings Scale
Introduction & Directions

All members of the family experience a wide variety of feelings when a breakup has been initiated. It is important to explore all of the feelings that both care-givers and children or teens are experiencing in the situation.

This scale can help you explore the specific feelings you are experiencing in this breakup, and provide exercises to help all family members resolve their feelings. This scale contains 24 statements. Read each of the statements and decide how descriptive each statement is of you or your family member. In each of the choices listed, circle the number of your response on the line to the right of each statement.

Examples

Scale # 1 and # 3 (Individual's responses)

In the following example, the circled number 1 under "RARELY" indicates the statement is rarely true of the person completing the scale.

	ALWAYS	SOMETIMES	RARELY/NEVER
I am more quiet than before	3	2	(1)

Scale # 2 and # 4: (Individual's perceptions)

In the following example, the circled number 2 under "SOMETIMES" indicates the person who is completing the scale believes that this statement is sometimes true about the other family member.

I believe this care-giver ...

	ALWAYS	SOMETIMES	RARELY/NEVER
is more quiet than before	3	(2)	1

This is not a test and there are no right or wrong answers. Do not spend too much time thinking about your answers. Your initial response will be the most true for you. Be sure to respond to every statement.

(Turn to the next page and begin.)

SCALE #1

Child's/Teen's *Feelings*

Child's/Teen's Name ______________________________ Date ______________

	ALWAYS	SOMETIMES	RARELY/NEVER
I am more quiet than before	3	2	1
I spend more time alone than before.	3	2	1
I am very sad	3	2	1
I have lost interest in things I used to enjoy	3	2	1
I keep everything inside	3	2	1
I cry easily	3	2	1

D TOTAL = ________

	ALWAYS	SOMETIMES	RARELY/NEVER
I feel like I have been let down	3	2	1
I feel that no one cares about what's good for me	3	2	1
I have anger outbursts for no good reason	3	2	1
I am disappointed and I let everyone know it	3	2	1
I am furious with my care-givers	3	2	1
I am very upset but I do not discuss it with anyone	3	2	1

A TOTAL = ________

	ALWAYS	SOMETIMES	RARELY/NEVER
I am afraid of what will happen	3	2	1
I fear that my care-givers will never get along again	3	2	1
I worry a lot	3	2	1
I am afraid that my care-givers don't care about me anymore	3	2	1
I don't want to be separated from my other care-giver	3	2	1
I worry that something might happen to the care-giver I live with	3	2	1

F TOTAL = ________

	ALWAYS	SOMETIMES	RARELY/NEVER
I believe the breakup is my fault	3	2	1
I don't understand what happened	3	2	1
I misbehaved and then my care-givers split up	3	2	1
I believe this is my care-givers way of punishing me	3	2	1
I feel guilty for what happened	3	2	1
I feel guilty because I am happy that they broke up	3	2	1

G TOTAL = ________

SCALE #1
Child's/Teen's *Feelings*
Scoring Directions

Child's/Teen's Name ______________________________ Date ______________

All family members experience a wide array of feelings when there is a breakup. It is important to be able to accept, express and manage all of these emotions. Add the numbers you circled on the four scales you just completed and write that score on the line marked Total. Then transfer that total to the space below.

D Depression **Total =** __________

A Anger **Total =** __________

F Fear **Total =** __________

G Guilt **Total =** __________

Profile Interpretation

Scale Score	Result	Indications
6 to 9	Low	Low Scores indicate that you have accepted, expressed, and managed the emotions related to your family breakup.
10 to 14	Moderate	Moderate Scores indicate that you have somewhat accepted, expressed, and managed the emotions related to your family breakup.
15 to 18	High	High Scores indicate that you have not accepted, expressed, and managed the emotions related to your family breakup.

Scale Descriptions

Depression – The child/teen scoring High on this scale feels sad, cries easily, and has lost interest in activities which were interesting in the past.

Anger – The child/teen scoring High on this scale feels angry, uncared about, and has been acting aggressively.

Fear – The child/teen scoring High on this scale is worried a lot of the time, feels unloved by one or both care-givers, and is afraid of what will happen in the future.

Guilt – The child/teen scoring High on this scale feels guilty about the breakup, believes they are at fault, and feels a sense of responsibility for the breakup.

SCALE #2

Child's/Teen's Perception of a Care-Giver's *Feelings*

Child's/Teen's Name ______________________________ Date ______________

Care-Giver's Name ____

I believe this care-giver ...	ALWAYS	SOMETIMES	RARELY/NEVER
is more quiet than before	3	2	1
spends more time alone than before	3	2	1
seems very sad	3	2	1
has lost interest in things he/she used to enjoy	3	2	1
keeps everything inside	3	2	1
cries easily	3	2	1

D TOTAL = ________

I believe this care-giver ...	ALWAYS	SOMETIMES	RARELY/NEVER
feels like he/she let me down	3	2	1
doesn't care about me	3	2	1
has angry outbursts for no good reasons	3	2	1
is disappointed and lets everyone know it	3	2	1
is furious	3	2	1
is very upset but doesn't discuss it with anyone	3	2	1

A TOTAL = ________

I believe this care-giver ...	ALWAYS	SOMETIMES	RARELY/NEVER
is afraid of what will happen	3	2	1
worries that he/she will not get along with the other care-giver	3	2	1
worries a lot	3	2	1
thinks that I don't care about her/him anymore	3	2	1
doesn't want to be separated from the children	3	2	1
worries that something might happen	3	2	1

F TOTAL = ________

I believe this care-giver ...	ALWAYS	SOMETIMES	RARELY/NEVER
takes the blame for the breakup	3	2	1
doesn't understand what happened	3	2	1
is worried the children will think something they did caused it	3	2	1
is worried that the children will think they are being punished.	3	2	1
feels guilty for what happened	3	2	1
feels guilty for being happy the relationship is over	3	2	1

G TOTAL = ________

SCALE #2
Child's/Teen's Perception of One Care-Giver's *Feelings*
Scoring Directions

Child's/Teen's Name ______________________________ Date ______________

Care-Giver's Name ____

All family members experience a wide array of feelings when parents break up. Therefore, it is important to be able to accept, express and manage all of these emotions. Add the numbers you circled on the four scales you just completed and write that score on the line marked Total. Then transfer that total to the space below.

D Depression **Total =** __________

A Anger **Total =** __________

F Fear **Total =** __________

G Guilt **Total =** __________

Profile Interpretation

Scale Score	Result	Indications
6 to 9	Low	Low Scores indicate that you believe this care-giver has accepted, expressed, and managed the emotions related to the family breakup.
10 to 14	Moderate	Moderate Scores indicate that you believe this care-giver has somewhat accepted, expressed, and managed the emotions related to the family breakup.
15 to 18	High	High Scores indicate that you believe this care-giver has not accepted, expressed, and managed the emotions related to the family breakup.

Scale Descriptions

Depression – The child or teen scoring High on this scale feels that the above stated care-giver is sad, cries easily, and has lost interest in activities which were interesting in the past.

Anger – The child or teen scoring High on this scale feels that the above stated care-giver feels angry, worries that the children feel neglected and unloved, and has been acting aggressively.

Fear – The child or teen scoring High on this scale feels that the above stated care-giver is worried a lot of the time, thinks the children may feel unloved, and is afraid of what will happen in the future.

Guilt – The child or teen scoring High on this scale feels that the above stated care-giver feels guilty about the breakup, feels at fault and a sense of responsibility for the breakup.

SCALE #3

Care-Giver's *Feelings*

Care-Giver's Name ______________________________ Date ____________

Child's/Teen's Name ______________________________

	ALWAYS	SOMETIMES	RARELY/NEVER
I am more quiet than before	3	2	1
I spend more time alone than before	3	2	1
I am very sad	3	2	1
I have lost interest in things I used to enjoy	3	2	1
I keep everything inside	3	2	1
I cry easily	3	2	1

D TOTAL = ________

	ALWAYS	SOMETIMES	RARELY/NEVER
I feel like I have been let down	3	2	1
I feel that no one cares about what's good for me	3	2	1
I have anger outbursts for no good reason	3	2	1
I am disappointed and I let everyone know it	3	2	1
I am furious with my ex	3	2	1
I am very upset but I do not discuss it with anyone	3	2	1

A TOTAL = ________

	ALWAYS	SOMETIMES	RARELY/NEVER
I am afraid of what will happen	3	2	1
I fear that my family will never get along again	3	2	1
I worry a lot	3	2	1
I am afraid that my family doesn't care about me anymore	3	2	1
I don't want to be separated from my ex	3	2	1
I worry that something bad might happen	3	2	1

F TOTAL = ________

	ALWAYS	SOMETIMES	RARELY/NEVER
I believe the breakup is my fault	3	2	1
I don't understand what happened	3	2	1
I didn't do the best I could	3	2	1
I believe I am being punished	3	2	1
I feel guilty for what happened	3	2	1
I feel guilty because I am happy that we broke up	3	2	1

G TOTAL = ________

SCALE #3
Care-Giver's *Feelings*
Scoring Directions

Care-Giver's Name ______________________ Date ____________

Child's/Teen's Name ______________________

All family members experience a wide array of feelings when there is a break up. Therefore, it is important to be able to accept, express and manage all of these emotions. Add the numbers you circled on the four scales you just completed and write that score on the line marked Total. Then transfer that total to the space below.

D Depression **Total =** ________

A Anger **Total =** ________

F Fear **Total =** ________

G Guilt **Total =** ________

Profile Interpretation

Scale Score	Result	Indications
6 to 9	Low	Low Scores indicate that you have very effectively accepted, expressed and are able to manage the emotions related with the family.
10 to 14	Moderate	Moderate Scores indicate that you have fairly effectively accepted, expressed and are managing the emotions related with the family breakup fairly well.
15 to 18	High	High Scores indicate that you have not effectively accepted, expressed and managed the emotions related with the family breakup.

Scale Descriptions

Depression – The care-giver scoring High on this scale feels sad, cries easily, and has lost interest in activities which were interesting in the past.

Anger – The care-giver scoring High on this scale feels angry, deserted by other family members, and has been acting aggressively.

Fear – The care-giver scoring High on this scale is worried a lot of the time, feels abandoned by other family members and fear of what will happen in the future.

Guilt – The care-giver scoring High on this scale feels guilty about the breakup, believes he/she is at fault, and feels responsible for the breakup.

SCALE #4

Care-Giver's Perception of a Child's/Teen's *Feelings*

Care-Giver's Name ________________________________ Date ____________

Child's/Teen's Name ____

I believe this child or teen …	**ALWAYS**	**SOMETIMES**	**RARELY/NEVER**
is more quiet than before	3	2	1
spends more time alone than before	3	2	1
seems very sad	3	2	1
has lost interest in things he/she used to enjoy	3	2	1
keeps everything inside	3	2	1
cries easily	3	2	1

D TOTAL = ________

I believe this child or teen …			
feels like he/she let me down	3	2	1
doesn't care about me	3	2	1
has angry outbursts for no good reasons	3	2	1
is disappointed and lets everyone know it	3	2	1
is furious	3	2	1
is very upset but doesn't discuss it with anyone	3	2	1

A TOTAL = ________

I believe this child or teen …			
is afraid of what will happen	3	2	1
is worried that the care-givers will never get along	3	2	1
worries a lot	3	2	1
thinks that I don't care about her/him anymore	3	2	1
doesn't want to be separated from the other care-giver	3	2	1
worries that something might happen	3	2	1

F TOTAL = ________

I believe this child or teen …			
feels as if the breakup is his/her fault	3	2	1
doesn't understand what happened	3	2	1
thinks he or she did something that caused it	3	2	1
thinks he or she is being punished	3	2	1
feels guilty for what happened	3	2	1
feels guilty for being happy the relationship is over	3	2	1

G TOTAL = ________

SCALE #4
Care-Giver's Perception of a Child's/Teen's *Feelings* Scoring Directions

Care-Giver's Name ______________________________ Date ______________

Child's/Teen's Name ____

All family members experience a wide array of feelings when parents breakup. Therefore, it is important to be able to accept, express and manage all of these emotions. Add the numbers you circled on the four scales you just completed and write that score on the line marked Total. Then transfer that total to the space below.

D Depression **Total =** ____________

A Anger **Total =** ____________

F Fear **Total =** ____________

G Guilt **Total =** ____________

Profile Interpretation

Scale Score	Result	Indications
6 to 9	Low	Low Scores indicate that you believe the above stated child or teen has accepted, expressed, and managed the emotions related to the family breakup.
10 to 14	Moderate	Moderate Scores indicate that you believe above stated child or teen has somewhat accepted, expressed, and managed the emotions related to the family breakup.
15 to 18	High	High Scores indicate that you believe above stated child or teen has not accepted, expressed, and managed the emotions related to the family breakup.

Scale Descriptions

Depression – The care-giver scoring High on this scale feels that the above stated child or teen is sad, cries easily, and has lost interest in activities which were interesting in the past.

Anger – The care-giver scoring High on this scale feels that the above stated child or teen feels angry, worries that he or she feels neglected, and has been acting aggressively.

Fear – The care-giver scoring High on this scale feels that the above stated child or teen is worried a lot of the time, thinks the children may feel unloved, and fears what will happen in the future.

Guilt – The care-giver scoring High on this scale feels that the above stated child or teen feels guilty about the breakup, feels at fault, and feels a sense of responsibility for the breakup.

Feelings Scale

Family Score Totals

For each of the items on the scales, insert the person's name completing the scale, and transfer each person's scale on one line below. This form can be helpful in allowing family members to compare their own results.

Scale 1 Name (Child's/Teen's Scale)	Score Depression	Score Anger	Score Fear	Score Guilt	TOTAL SCORE
Example: *John*	*12*	*15*	*8*	*16*	*51*

Scale 2 Name (Child's/Teen's Perception of Care-Giver Scale)	Score Depression	Score Anger	Score Fear	Score Guilt	TOTAL SCORE

Scale 3 Name (Care-Giver's Scale)	Score Depression	Score Anger	Score Fear	Score Guilt	TOTAL SCORE

Scale 4 Name (Care-Giver's Perception of Child's/Teen's Scale)	Score Depression	Score Anger	Score Fear	Score Guilt	TOTAL SCORE

New Opportunities

Breakups can be frustrating, but they also can provide you with a variety of new opportunities that can give you many new things to look forward to. In the spaces that follow, list some of the new opportunities you can see as possibilities.

The Change	Possible Opportunities	How it Will Work Out Well

Which opportunity do you think is the most significant? Why?

It's Okay to Have Feelings

In the space below, write or draw your feelings about the breakup.

The Breakup Grieving Process

Regardless of their makeup and family dynamics, some members of a family usually proceed through some or all of the grief stages as they progress through a breakup. It is helpful to recognize, determine, and understand where in this process you, and possibly each member of the family, are functioning.

Place a ☑ in the box that describes the stage that you can identify being in right now.
Place an ☒ in the stage you have already gone through.
Leave the box blank ☐ if you haven't gone through the stage.
(You can be in more than one stage at a time. There may be some stages you will not experience.)

Stage 1 Denial

☐ People pretend that the breakup is not a big deal and that people can easily move on with their lives. They often talk about their situation and their emotions until the initial shock wears off. Most people in this stage feel numb about the situation and try to quickly move passed it.

Stage 2 Anger

☐ People begin to become angry about their situation or others involved in the breakup. They get angry and see themselves as victims of an injustice. In this stage, the anger can range from mild feelings of aggravation to feelings of rage. People often search for ways to vent their anger.

Stage 3 Bargaining

☐ People try different tactics to get back what they had. They begin to believe that a reconciliation, no matter how bad the situation was, is better than living without the partner or couple. They often seek a "quick fix" for the situation so that they can get back to the way life was before, even if it was not ideal. In this stage, many members of the family will feel guilty about what happened.

Stage 4 Sadness

☐ People begin to experience signs of sadness, often leading to depression. They may have difficulty sleeping, lose interest in eating, and feel exhausted or irritated. People feel sad and wish the relationship had turned out differently.

Stage 5 Moving On

☐ People begin to accept the fact that a breakup might be the best for some or all of the people in the relationship, and they are ready to move on. They are interested in releasing the past, living in the moment, and making strides toward a fulfilling future. They realize that it is time to move on and focus on the good people and pleasant and rewarding aspects of their lives.

Stage 6 Release & Establishment

☐ In this stage, people are ready to release any bitterness and even accept the reality of the situation. They are ready to begin establishing new relationships that will part of a positive future.

Under each stage, put the family member's name of the one you perceive going through that stage right now.

Early Warning Signs

It is important to be aware of some of the early warning signs of negative emotions that you may be experiencing related to the breakup. In the spaces that follow, identify some of the ways you know you are experiencing the feelings listed. *(Example: tears, tense body, clenched teeth, clinched fists, heavy breathing, stomach ache, outbursts, etc.)*

Feelings	How I Know I am Experiencing This Feeling	How I Can Reduce These Negative Emotions
Anger		
Fear		
Guilt		
Emptyness		
Loneliness		
Jealousy		
Hatred		
Sadness		
Other		
Other		

Owning & Naming Emotions

It is normal to experience a variety of emotions during and after a breakup, but it is also important to acknowledge and identify these feelings. Draw faces of the feelings you experience most.

Keeping your feelings in will intensify them and prolong your negativity!

Who can you talk with? ____

Ways to Express Negative Emotions

One of the best ways for families to deal with the stress of change is to accept the fact that they are in the midst of a change and find ways to face it, not to avoid it or deny it. How can you begin to express your negative emotions in a healthy way? *(Example: leave, stop and breathe deeply, physical activity, etc.)*

Situation	Negative Emotions I Experience	How I Will Express Them in A Healthy Way
Example: *I had to move to a new school*	*Anger, and frustration.*	*Join a basketball team.*

Which emotion do you experience most? How will you now manage the emotion?

____

____

____

Both Types of Emotions

In a breakup, all members of the family usually experience a wide variety of emotions. Some of these emotions are positive and some are negative. In the spaces that follow, identify some of the positive emotions you have about the breakup. For example, you may think, "I'm glad mom will get away from the abuse. She might be content again." or "Our home is calmer now."

Positive Thought About the Breakup	Emotion	How Life Will Be Different

Next, think about the negative emotions you are experiencing. In the spaces that follow, identify some of the negative emotions you are experiencing. For example, you may think, "I'm angry that I can't go to ballgames with both care-givers!" or "I'm happy I can enjoy watching my child play."

Negative Thought About the Breakup	Emotion	How Life Will Be Different

Talk With Others

It is important to talk with others about your feelings related to the breakup. Below, identify a person with whom you might talk with about your negative emotions. Describe how he or she can help you, and how you can approach each person.

A Person With Whom I Can Talk	How This Person Can Help Me	Ways I Can Approach this Person
Example: *Bob*	*He is a great listener.*	*I will make arrangements with him to see him and will talk to him then.*

Journaling Prompts

Complete each of the journal prompts to further explore your feelings related to the breakup.

I feel ____

____

____.

When ____,
I feel ____

____.

When I feel ____,
I want to ____

____.

I would rather ____

____

____.

I get so ____,
that I ____

____.

The positive feeling I have the most often is ______________________________

____

____.

The most negative feeling I have the most often is ______________________________

____

____.

When I feel ____,
I can't ____

____.

When I feel ____,
I want to ____

____.

Red Flags!

You need to be aware of the red flags *(warnings)* that may be pointing toward a more serious emotional problem. In the spaces that follow, identify any emotional red flags you may be experiencing.

Red Flags	How I Experience This	Person With Whom I Can Talk
Sleep Problems		
Eating Problems		
Self-Injury		
Substance Abuse		
Acts of Violence		
Withdrawal from Family/Friends		
Lack of Interest in Activities		
Suicidal Thoughts		
Feelings of Worthlessness		
Irritability		
Physical Complaints		
Other		

Let's Be Honest

People often are reluctant to share their honest feelings with one another for fear that they will offend or hurt someone. Following a family breakup, it is important to honestly express feelings toward family members. In the spaces below, tell members of the family how you feel about them or their actions.

Family Member	How I Feel Right Now	Why I Feel this Way	What I Can Say to this Person
Example: *Daughter*	*Devastated.*	*She will not talk to me or see me.*	*I understand how you feel but I am hurting too. Can we please get together alone or with a counselor to talk about it?*

Why is it sometimes so difficult to be honest?

____

____

____

____

Guilt about the Family Change

Think about the change or changes that are currently occurring in your family. Do you feel any guilt about what the family is experiencing? If so, journal about it below.

I wish I had …
I feel like I …
I regret …
I can change or control …
I …

Illogical Thoughts & Feelings

Illogical thoughts can perpetuate your negativity and escalate the negative feelings with other family members. Many of the negative feelings you have about the family breakup are related to illogical thoughts. In the spaces that follow, identify the negative thoughts you are experiencing related to the breakup. Then explore the emotions tied to these thoughts and the results of your negative emotions.

The Thoughts that are in My Head	When I Think this, I feel ...	Then I ...
Example: *Dad could have tried harder.*	*Angry and resentful. I blame him.*	*Tell my sisters that Dad could have tried harder. Then we're all angry. (And really, he probably did try.)*

What trends do you see? ____

What steps can you take to reduce or change the thoughts that lead to negative emotions?

CHAPTER IV

Changes

For the Facilitator

Explanation of the Four Scales in this Chapter

As the facilitator, you may choose any combination of assessments that will work for each of the particular families with whom you are working.

You may choose to use one scale or all of them, depending on the make-up of the family and the number of people in the family.

Photocopy as many of each as needed.

1. **One for each child/teen** to identify personal feelings
2. **One for each child/teen** to identify perceptions of care-giver's feelings
3. **One for each adult** to identify personal feelings
4. **One for each adult** to identify perceptions of children's or teens' feelings

You will need to photocopy the corresponding Introduction and Directions for each scale you administer.

Chapter IV – *Changes* Skills

These skills are behavioral objectives which family members will meet as they engage in the assessments and guided self-exploration activities.

Children/Teens

Self-assess, score, and interpret personal feelings, and perception of care-givers' feelings on three scales: lifestyle, finances, and differences.

Identify likes and dislikes regarding involvements and activities with each care-giver.

Describe expectations for self, family members, care-givers, life changes, etc.

Care-Givers

Self-assess, score, and interpret personal feelings, and perception of children/teens' feelings on three scales: lifestyle, finances, and differences.

Define aspects of the new relationship with the ex-partner, and ways children will benefit from consistency, rules, conflict resolution, etc. State what to do about areas of disagreement.

All Family Members

Compare individual results with other family members, and the family's total scores on three scales: lifestyle, finances, and differences.

Identify the impact of change by sharing likes and dislikes regarding a list of expected changes.

Point out one's biggest concern and give reasons.

Describe new and old traditions to keep regarding meals, birthdays, holidays, activities, school, etc.

Identify new routines to establish regarding technology, chores, pets, work, quiet time, etc.

Describe regrets, whether realistic or unrealistic, and people who can help clarify this.

Personalize words of wisdom by specifying ways to reconstruct the future and the positive aspects of starting over.

Depict and/or describe one's imagined life five years from now. Include details about residence, activities, interpersonal contacts, etc.

Changes Scale
Introduction & Directions

Following any breakup, there are many changes, some positive, some negative. It is important to examine and explore the impact (or potential impact) that these changes will have on all of the family members.

This assessment contains 18 statements. Read each of the statements and decide how descriptive the statement is of you or your family members. In each of the choices listed, circle the number of your response on the line to the right of each statement.

Examples

Scale # 1 and # 3 (Individual's responses)

In the following example, the circled number 3 indicates that the statement is a somewhat descriptive of the person completing the scale.

4 = Very Descriptive 3 = Somewhat Descriptive 2 = A Little Descriptive 1 = Not At All

In our family ...

The structure is different . . . . 4 . . . . (3) 2 1

Scale # 2 and # 4: (Individual's perceptions)

In the following example, the circled number 1 indicates the person who is completing the scale perceives that it is not at all descriptive about the other family member.

In our family, I believe the care-giver thinks ...

The structure is different . . . . 4 . . . . . 3 . . . . . 2 . . . . (1)

This is not a test and there are no right or wrong answers. Do not spend too much time thinking about your answers. Your initial response will be the most true for you. Be sure to respond to every statement.

(Turn to the next page and begin.)

SCALE #1

Child's/Teen's *Changes*

Child's/Teen's Name ______________________________ Date ______________

4 = Very Descriptive 3 = Somewhat Descriptive 2 = A Little Descriptive 1 = Not At All

Within my family ...

The structure is different. . . . . 4 . . . . 3 . . . . 2 1
The routine is different . . . . 4 . . . . 3 . . . . 2 1
The time my care-givers spend with me is different . . . . 4 . . . . 3 . . . . 2 1
The traditions are different . . . . 4 . . . . 3 . . . . 2 1
No one cares about what I want . . . . 4 . . . . 3 . . . . 2 1
My world is very different now. . . . . 4 . . . . 3 . . . . 2 1

L TOTAL = ________

Within my family ...

We have less money than before . . . . 4 . . . . 3 . . . . 2 1
We don't have enough money. . . . . 4 . . . . 3 . . . . 2 1
My primary care-giver will not be able to buy extras or
some necessities anymore . . . . 4 . . . . 3 . . . . 2 1
We will have less than we did before. . . . . 4 . . . . 3 . . . . 2 1
We will not be able to do things we want to do . . . . 4 . . . . 3 . . . . 2 1
We may need to move to a less expensive place to live . . . . 4 . . . . 3 . . . . 2 1

F TOTAL = ________

Within my family ...

We're not a real family anymore . . . . 4 . . . . 3 . . . . 2 1
Activities will be different . . . . 4 . . . . 3 . . . . 2 1
I have trouble adjusting to the family differences . . . . 4 . . . . 3 . . . . 2 1
I am worried because everything will be different. . . . . 4 . . . . 3 . . . . 2 1
I do not want a different family. I want my old one . . . . 4 . . . . 3 . . . . 2 1
We will not see one or all of our family members again . . . . 4 . . . . 3 . . . . 2 1

D TOTAL = ________

SCALE #1
Child's/Teen's *Changes*
Scoring Directions

Child's/Teen's Name ______________________________ Date ____________

The assessment you just completed is designed to measure how well you are dealing with the changes associated with a breakup. For each of the items on the previous page, count the scores you circled. Put that total on the line marked Total at the end of the assessment. Then, transfer your total to the spaces below. Add your three scores to get your Grand Total.

L Life Style Total = __________

F Finances Total = __________

D Differences Total = __________

GRAND TOTAL = __________

Profile Interpretation

Scale Score	Grand Total	Result	Indications
6 to 10	18 to 28	Low	Low scores indicate that you are not very worried about the changes that are occurring in your family due to the breakup.
11 to 16	29 to 45	Moderate	Moderate scores indicate that you are somewhat worried about the changes that are occurring in your family due to the breakup.
17 to 24	46 to 72	High	High scores indicate that you are extremely worried about the changes that are occurring in your family due to the breakup.

Scale Descriptions

Life Style – A child or teen scoring High on this scale is quite concerned about the changes in routines, structure and traditions.

Finances – A child or teen scoring High on this scale is quite concerned about how the financial issues will affect him or her and the family.

Differences – A child or teen scoring High on this scale is quite concerned about how the family will operate in different ways.

GRAND TOTAL - A child or teen scoring HIGH on the total of all three scales indicates that he or she believes that the family is experiencing significant changes and is worried about the effect of all these changes on all of their life style, finances.

SCALE #2

Child's/Teen's Perception of a Care-Giver's *Changes*

Child's/Teen's Name ______________________________ Date ______________

Care-Giver's Name ______________________________

4 = Very Descriptive 3 = Somewhat Descriptive 2 = A Little Descriptive 1 = Not At All

In our family, I believe this care-giver thinks ...

The structure is different . . . . . 4 . . . . 3 . . . . 2 1
The routine is different . . . . . 4 . . . . 3 . . . . 2 1
The time we spend together is different . . . . . 4 . . . . 3 . . . . 2 1
The traditions are different . . . . . 4 . . . . 3 . . . . 2 1
No one cares about what I want . . . . . 4 . . . . 3 . . . . 2 1
My world is very different now . . . . . 4 . . . . 3 . . . . 2 1

L TOTAL = ________

In our family, I believe this care-giver thinks ...

We have less money than before . . . . . 4 . . . . 3 . . . . 2 1
We don't have enough money . . . . . 4 . . . . 3 . . . . 2 1
We will not be able to buy extras or some necessities anymore . . . . . 4 . . . . 3 . . . . 2 1
We will have less than we did before . . . . . 4 . . . . 3 . . . . 2 1
We will not be able to do things we want to do . . . . . 4 . . . . 3 . . . . 2 1
We may need to move to a less expensive place to live . . . . . 4 . . . . 3 . . . . 2 1

F TOTAL = ________

In our family, I believe this care-giver thinks ...

We're not a real family anymore . . . . . 4 . . . . 3 . . . . 2 1
Activities will be different . . . . . 4 . . . . 3 . . . . 2 1
We will have trouble adjusting to the family differences . . . . . 4 . . . . 3 . . . . 2 1
I am worried because everything will be different . . . . . 4 . . . . 3 . . . . 2 1
I do not want a different family, I want the old one . . . . . 4 . . . . 3 . . . . 2 1
We will not see one or all of our family members again . . . . . 4 . . . . 3 . . . . 2 1

D TOTAL = ________

SCALE #2
Child's/Teen's Perception of One Care-Giver's *Changes*
Scoring Directions

Child's/Teen's Name ______________________________ Date ______________

Care-Giver's Name ____

The assessment you just completed is designed to measure how you perceive a care-giver in your life feels about the changes associated with a breakup. For each of the items on the previous pages, count the scores you circled. Put that total on the line marked Total at the end of the scale. Then, transfer your total to the space below. Add your three scores to get your Grand Total.

L Life Style **Total** = __________

F Finances **Total** = __________

D Differences **Total** = __________

GRAND TOTAL = __________

Profile Interpretation

Scale Score	Scale Score	Result	Indications
6 to 10	18 to 28	Low	Low scores indicate that you perceive the above stated care-giver is not very worried about the changes that are occurring in your family due to the breakup.
11 to 16	29 to 45	Moderate	Moderate scores indicate that you perceive the above stated care-giver is somewhat worried about the changes that are occurring in your family due to the breakup.
17 to 24	46 to 72	High	High scores indicate that you perceive the above stated care-giver is extremely worried about the changes that are occurring in your family due to the breakup.

Scale Descriptions

Life Style – The child or teen scoring High on this scale perceives that the above stated care-giver is quite concerned about the changes in routines, structure and traditions.

Finances – The child or teen scoring High on this scale perceives that the above stated care-giver is quite concerned about how the financial issues will affect them and the family.

Differences – The child or teen scoring High on this scale perceives that the above stated care-giver is quite concerned about how the family will operate in different ways.

GRAND TOTAL - The child or teen scoring HIGH on the total of all three scales perceives that the above stated care-giver believes that the family is experiencing significant changes and is worried about the effect of all these changes on their life style, finances, and differences.

SCALE #3
Care-Giver's *Changes*

Care-Giver's Name ________________________________ Date ______________

4 = Very Descriptive 3 = Somewhat Descriptive 2 = A Little Descriptive 1 = Not At All

In our family ...

The structure is different . . . . 4 . . . . 3 . . . . 2 1
The routine is different . . . . 4 . . . . 3 . . . . 2 1
The time I spend with my children is different . . . . 4 . . . . 3 . . . . 2 1
The traditions are different . . . . 4 . . . . 3 . . . . 2 1
No one cares about what I want . . . . 4 . . . . 3 . . . . 2 1
My world is very different now . . . . 4 . . . . 3 . . . . 2 1

L TOTAL = ________

In our family ...

We have less money than before . . . . 4 . . . . 3 . . . . 2 1
We don't have enough money . . . . 4 . . . . 3 . . . . 2 1
We will not be able to buy extras or some necessities anymore . . . . 4 . . . . 3 . . . . 2 1
We will have less than we did before . . . . 4 . . . . 3 . . . . 2 1
We will not be able to do things we want to do . . . . 4 . . . . 3 . . . . 2 1
We may need to move to a less expensive place to live . . . . 4 . . . . 3 . . . . 2 1

F TOTAL = ________

In our family ...

We're not a real family anymore . . . . 4 . . . . 3 . . . . 2 1
Activities will be different . . . . 4 . . . . 3 . . . . 2 1
I have trouble adjusting to the family differences . . . . 4 . . . . 3 . . . . 2 1
I am worried because everything will be different . . . . 4 . . . . 3 . . . . 2 1
I do not want a different family. I want my old one . . . . 4 . . . . 3 . . . . 2 1
We will not see one or all of our family members again . . . . 4 . . . . 3 . . . . 2 1

D TOTAL = ________

SCALE #3
Care-Giver's *Changes*
Scoring Directions

Care-Giver's Name ______________________________ Date ______________

The assessment you just completed is designed to measure how well you are dealing with the changes associated with a breakup. For each of the items on the previous pages, count the scores you circled. Put that total on the line marked Total at the end of the assessment. Then, transfer your total to the space below. Add your three scores to get your Grand Total.

L Life Style Total = ___________

F Finances Total = ___________

D Differences Total = ___________

GRAND TOTAL = ___________

Profile Interpretation

Scale Score	Scale Score	Result	Indications
6 to 10	18 to 28	Low	Low scores indicate that you are not very worried about the changes that are occurring in your family due to the breakup.
11 to 16	29 to 45	Moderate	Moderate scores indicate that you are somewhat worried about the changes that are occurring in your family due to the breakup.
17 to 24	46 to 72	High	High scores indicate that you are extremely worried about the changes that are occurring in your family due to the breakup.

Scale Descriptions

Life Style – The care-giver scoring High on this scale are quite concerned about the changes in routines, structure and traditions.

Finances – The care-giver scoring High on this scale are quite concerned about how the financial issues will affect them and the family.

Differences – The care-giver scoring High on this scale are quite concerned about how the family will operate in different ways.

GRAND TOTAL - People scoring HIGH on the total of all three scales indicates that they believe that their family is experiencing significant changes and they are worried about the effect of all these changes on their life style, finances, and differences.

SCALE #4

Care-Giver's Perception of a Child's/Teen's *Changes*

Care-Giver's Name ____ Date ________________

Child's/Teen's Name ____

4 = Very Descriptive **3 = Somewhat Descriptive** **2 = A Little Descriptive** **1 = Not At All**

In our family, I believes this child/teen thinks ...

The structure is different. . . . . .4. . . . .3. . . . .2. 1
The routine is different . . . . .4. . . . .3. . . . .2. 1
The time my care-givers spend with me is different . . . . .4. . . . .3. . . . .2. 1
The traditions are different . . . . .4. . . . .3. . . . .2. 1
No one cares about what I want . . . . .4. . . . .3. . . . .2. 1
My world is very different now. . . . . .4. . . . .3. . . . .2. 1

L TOTAL = ________

In our family, I believes this child/teen thinks ...

We have less money than before . . . . .4. . . . .3. . . . .2. 1
We don't have enough money. . . . . .4. . . . .3. . . . .2. 1
We will not be able to buy extras or some necessities anymore . . . . .4. . . . .3. . . . .2. 1
We will have less than we did before. . . . . .4. . . . .3. . . . .2. 1
We will not be able to do things we want to do . . . . .4. . . . .3. . . . .2. 1
We may need to move to a less expensive place to live . . . . .4. . . . .3. . . . .2. 1

F TOTAL = ________

In our family, I believes this child/teen thinks ...

We're not a real family anymore . . . . .4. . . . .3. . . . .2. 1
Activities will be different . . . . .4. . . . .3. . . . .2. 1
I have trouble adjusting to the family differences . . . . .4. . . . .3. . . . .2. 1
I am worried because everything will be different. . . . . .4. . . . .3. . . . .2. 1
I do not want a different family. I want my old one . . . . .4. . . . .3. . . . .2. 1
We will not see one or all of our family members again . . . . .4. . . . .3. . . . .2. 1

D TOTAL = ________

SCALE #4
Care-Giver's Perception of a Child's/Teen's *Changes*
Scoring Directions

Care-Giver's Name _______________________________ Date ____________

Child's/Teen's Name ____

The assessment you just completed is designed to measure how you perceive a child or care-giver in your life feels about the changes associated with a breakup. For each of the items on the previous pages, count the scores you circled. Put that total on the line marked Total at the end of the scale. Then, transfer your total to the space below. Add your three scores to get your Grand Total.

L Life Style **Total** = ____________

F Finances **Total** = ____________

D Differences **Total** = ____________

GRAND TOTAL = ____________

Profile Interpretation

Scale Score	Scale Score	Result	Indications
6 to 10	18 to 28	Low	Low scores indicate that you perceive the above stated child or teen is not very worried about the changes that are occurring in your family due to the breakup.
11 to 16	29 to 45	Moderate	Moderate scores indicate that you perceive the above stated child or teen is worried about the changes that are occurring in your family due to the breakup.
17 to 24	46 to 72	High	High scores indicate that you perceive the above stated child or teen is extremely worried about the changes that are occurring in your family due to the breakup.

Scale Descriptions

Life Style – The care-giver scoring High on this scale perceives that the above stated child or teen is quite concerned about the changes in routines, structure and traditions.

Finances – The care-giver scoring High on this scale perceives that the above stated child or teen is quite concerned about how the financial issues will affect them and the family.

Differences – The care-giver scoring High on this scale perceives that the above stated child or teen is quite concerned about how the family will operate in different ways.

GRAND TOTAL - The above stated care-giver scoring HIGH on the total of all three scales perceives that the above stated child or teen believes that the family is experiencing significant changes and is worried about the effect of all these changes on their life style, finances, and differences.

Changes Scale
Family Score Totals

For each of the items on the scales, insert the person's name completing the scale, and transfer each person's scale on one line below. This form can be helpful in allowing family members to compare their own results.

Scale 1 Name (Child's/Teen's Scale)	Score Life Style	Score Finances	Score Differences	TOTAL SCORE
Example: *John*	*20*	*18*	*12*	*50*

Scale 2 Name (Child's/Teen's Perception of Care-giver Scale)	Score Life Style	Score Finances	Score Differences	TOTAL SCORE

Scale 3 Name (Care-giver's Scale)	Score Life Style	Score Finances	Score Differences	TOTAL SCORE

Scale 4 Name (Care-giver's Perception of Child's/Teen's Scale)	Score Life Style	Score Finances	Score Differences	TOTAL SCORE

Ways Life is Different

A breakup brings on a variety of changes for care-givers and children. Some of these changes can be stressful, while others can be great! In the spaces that follow, identify some of the changes you will be experiencing and the impact you expect these changes to have on you.

Ways Life is or Will be Different	What I Like about the Difference	What I Don't Like About the Difference
Everyday Care		
Home		
My Other Home		
Family		
Friends		
Holidays		
Home		
Routine		
School or Work		
Spirituality / Religion		
Vacation / Camp		
Other		

What is your biggest concern and why? ____________________

____

____

Traditions

In each breakup, there will be changes in the family traditions. This can be stressful for some family members and not for others. It is important to create new traditions when possible and keep some of the old established traditions. In the spaces that follow, identify some of the new traditions you might like for your family to create. Identify which traditions you'd like to keep, if possible. Place an N next to a new tradition and an O next to an old tradition.

Birthdays and Family Celebrations	Meals
Holidays	**School-Related Activities**
Other	**Other**

Routines

In each breakup, there will be changes to the usual routines. It is important to re-establish new routines when possible. In the spaces that follow, write about the new routines you might like.

Time to Eat and with Whom	Bed Times and Routines
TV, Cell Phones, Electronic Games, etc.	School or Job Work at Home
Household Chores	Quiet Time
Bath and Hygiene Time	Extra Curriculum
Caring for Pets	Time for Social Life
Other	Other

Family Togetherness

(Child or Teen)

When children have two care-givers, they often need to work at being a part (or sometimes two parts) of a strong family unit. One way to do this is by identifying the things you do when you are with each care-giver, and how you feel about it. In the spaces that follow, identify what you do together with each care-giver when you are with them. *(**Examples:** play games, watch a movie, participate in family meetings, enjoy certain TV shows, eat meals together, eat meals alone, vacation, attend a house of worship, mow the grass, take out the garbage, visit with other family members, make sleep arrangements, etc.).*

Care-giver # 1 ______________________________

Our Involvements	What I Like to Do and Why	What I Don't Like to Do and Why

Care-giver # 2 ______________________________

Our Involvements	What I Like to Do and Why	What I Don't Like to Do and Why

Expectations of the Future

(Child or Teen)

It is important to think about your expectations for your future life with the family you live with. In the spaces that follow, explore some of your expectations. (If you split your time with more than one care-giver, complete this page for each one.)

Name ______________________ **Care-giver's Name** ______________________

I expect our family to ____

____

____

I expect that I will____

____

____

I expect that my life will change in the following ways ______________________

____

____

I expect that other family members will ______________________

____

____

I expect the care-giver I live with will ______________________

____

____

I expect the care-giver I don't live with will ______________________

____

____

I expect to be ____

____

____

Regret

Members of any family often have regrets after a parental breakup. In the spaces that follow, identify some of your regrets and explore whether or not they are realistic.

Regret #1:

Do you think this is realistic?

With whom can you discuss whether this is realistic or unrealistic?

Regret #2:

Do you think this is realistic?

With whom can you discuss whether this is realistic or unrealistic?

Regret #3:

Do you think this is realistic?

With whom can you discuss whether this is realistic or unrealistic?

Regret #4:

Do you think this is realistic?

With whom can you discuss whether this is realistic or unrealistic?

A New Relationship

(Care-Giver)

You may need to define a new relationship with your ex-partner to ensure that you do the best possible for your children. What will this new relationship look like?

Aspects of New Relationship	What We Can Do About This	How This Will Help Our Children
Consistency		
Communication		
Avoid negative talk about each other		
Rules		
Schedules		
Finances		
Compromise		
Resolving Conflicts		
Support		
New Relationships		

Which aspects are you unable to come to agreement about? What can you do about it?

____

____

Reconstruct Your Future

> *Today is a great day to reconstruct your future!*
> *Starting over beats staying put any day!*
>
> ~ Author Unknown

What does the above quote mean to you?

____

____

____

____

____

____

How would you like to reconstruct your future? Be specific.

____

____

____

____

____

____

What are the positive aspects of starting over?

____

____

____

____

____

____

Projecting into the Future

In the space that follows, draw a picture or write about what your life might look like in five years.
(Examples: Where will you be living? What will you be doing? Who will you be in contact with?)